Warwick Studies in Industrial Relations

Piecework Bargaining

Warwick Studies in Industrial Relations

General Editors: George Bain, Hugh Clegg,
Allan Flanders

Piecework Bargaining

William Brown

Social Science Research Council Industrial Relations Research Unit, University of Warwick

HEINEMANN EDUCATIONAL BOOKS
LONDON

Heinemann Educational Books Ltd

LONDON   EDINBURGH   MELBOURNE   AUCKLAND   TORONTO
HONG KONG   SINGAPORE   KUALA LUMPUR
IBADAN   NAIROBI   JOHANNESBURG
NEW DELHI

ISBN 435 85125 X

First published 1973

Published by
Heinemann Educational Books Ltd
48 Charles Street, London W1X 8AH

Printed in Great Britain by
Willmer Brothers Limited, Birkenhead

Editors' Foreword

Warwick University's first undergraduates were admitted in 1965. The teaching of industrial relations began a year later, and in 1967 a one-year graduate course leading to an M.A. in Industrial Relations was introduced. At about the same time a grant from the Clarkson Trustees allowed a beginning to be made on a research project concerned with several aspects of industrial relations in selected Coventry plants.

In 1970 the Social Science Research Council established three Research Units, one of them being the Industrial Relations Research Unit at Warwick. The Unit took over the Coventry project and developed others, including studies of union growth, union organisation, occupational labour markets, coloured immigrants in industry, ideologies of 'fairness' in industrial relations and the effects of the Industrial Relations Act.

This monograph series is intended to form the main vehicle for the publication of the results of the Unit's projects, of the research carried out by staff teaching industrial relations in the University, and, where it merits publication, of the work of graduate students. Some of these results will, of course, be published as articles, and some in the end may constitute full-scale volumes. But the monograph is the most apt form for much of our work. Industrial relations research is concerned with assembling and analysing evidence much of which cannot be succinctly summarized in tables and graphs, so that an adequate presentation of findings can easily take too much space for an article. On the other hand, even with a major project which will in the end lead to one or more books, there is often an advantage in publishing interim results as monographs. This is particularly true where the project deals, as do several of the industrial relations studies at Warwick, with problems of current interest for which employers, trade unionists and governments are anxiously seeking solutions.

This study of piecework bargaining by Mr Brown is a product of the Coventry project, started under the Clarkson grant and continued in the Industrial Relations Research Unit. It is therefore a companion to Dr Hyman's study of the working of the Engineering Disputes Procedure in Coventry (the first monograph in this series), but, like Dr Hyman's work, its significance extends far beyond Coventry. Five of the ten firms studied by Mr Brown are outside the Coventry area, and many of the features and tendencies which he describes are inherent in any piecework system. Moreover, as he argues, the 'hot-house' conditions of piecework provide a particularly favourable opportunity for examining the characteristics of systems of informal bargaining in general. Mr Brown shows that the movement and distribution of piecework earnings cannot be explained by the level of economic activity or changes in productivity. They are, he says, 'political phenomena to be understood through political analysis of the processes of collective bargaining.' Of paramount importance in most of the factories he studied were the 'custom and practice' rules governing the operation of piecework, and he examines the rules themselves and the ways in which they change. The rules vary with the strength and unity of the shop steward organization in the plant, but the main influence upon the shop steward organization is the control system operated by management, in its turn largely governed by the characteristics of the product market within which the firm competes. This is a major contribution to the theory of wage determination.

GEORGE BAIN
HUGH CLEGG
ALLAN FLANDERS

Contents

Acknowledgements

The research for this study required me to take up the time of large numbers of managers and trade unionists. My gratitude to these many individuals is all the greater for the kindness and patience with which they answered my questions. Mr Alan Berry of the Coventry and District Engineering Employers' Association, Mr Frank Chater of the Amalgamated Union of Engineering Workers, and Mr Bill Lapworth of the Transport and General Workers' Union and their colleagues also provided help and comments that are greatly appreciated. I am indebted to many academic colleagues. Fred Bayliss, John Corina, Rodney Crossley, Margaret Lawson and James Stern have all been generous with encouragement and advice. Within Warwick University, colleagues have been unfailingly helpful and have benefited this study from the very start. I am particularly grateful to Michael Mellish who worked with me on several of the case studies. The profoundest influence upon my research has been that of Hugh Clegg for whose supervision I have nothing but thanks.

to
my parents

Introduction

This is primarily a study of workshop bargaining under piecework payment systems in the engineering industry. The central problem is that of understanding wage determination when the operation of market forces is hampered or obscured by the exercise of bargaining power. An understanding of the use of power implies an understanding of the political processes through which it operates. Yet, despite morbid public interest in the more dramatic manifestations of plant bargaining, almost nothing is known about the politics of every-day behaviour within factories.

Piecework bargaining is of particular interest for two reasons. In the first place, it has long been suggested that piecework 'wage drift' leads rather than follows other wage movements and that it, as it were, primes the pump of wage inflation. Secondly, the continuous bargaining that occurs under piecework provides hot-house conditions under which the characteristics of informal bargaining emerge with unusual luxuriance. Consequently, although in some industries piecework is increasingly being replaced by alternative methods of payment, it can be argued that the insights it provides into wage determination and workplace industrial relations have a much wider relevance.

This account begins with a description of the principles and practice of piecework. It then considers the importance to piecework wage determination of two economic variables: the level of activity and the rate of increase of productivity. After this, attention turns to the way in which internal wage structures develop under piecework and to the forces influencing this development. A parallel consideration of the 'rules' governing the conduct of bargaining then demands a similar consideration of the way in which these rules emerge and change. Finally, the study makes a tentative attempt to analyse the political pressures bearing upon shop stewards and the controls operated by management.

The research is based on case studies of varying intensity in ten engineering factories. Five were in Coventry, four in the Birmingham area, and one in London. They were selected to provide a broad spread of production technologies and of bargaining activity. The research was carried out over several years and mostly involved the examination of wage data and documents and the unstructured interviewing of shop stewards, foremen, and managers. Even the fond eye of hindsight could not discern any rigorous method in the conduct of these studies. As in most research of this type, the questions that were both interesting and capable of investigation became apparent only gradually. Because it was often impossible to return to factories visited earlier in the study, some matters could not be looked at systematically for all ten cases. In addition, the availability of data and the facilities for interviews varied enormously between plants. But these problems are probably common to all comparative studies of workplace industrial relations.

I

Piecework in Theory and Practice

In recent years piecework has become the most abused of payment systems. It has been diagnosed as an aggravator of wage inflation, a provoker of strikes and an anathema to orderly industrial relations. Certainly, the more extreme forms of piecework bargaining are remarkable by any standards. The bargains that are continually in progress between individual workers and junior managers are often likened to the haggling of an oriental market, and the apparent absence of guidelines, combined with the frequent use of sanctions by workers, appears to place management in an unusually feeble position. Further, at least in the engineering industry, piecework appears often to provide exceptionally high earnings. At many of the highest paying factories in the country, as much as three-quarters of piece-work earnings' increases since the War have come as if by stealth, without conscious management decision or explicit negotiation.

As a prelude to an analysis of this remarkable bargaining process, this chapter sets out to explain the principles of piecework and why it can degenerate into what is often described as total 'anarchy'.

The Basic Principles of Piecework[1]

Approximately one half of manual workers in the British

[1] A survey of the literature on payment by results is given in National Board for Prices and Incomes, Report No 65, *Payment by Results*, Supplement, London: HMSO, Cmnd 3627, 1967. R. Marriot,

engineering industry are paid by results[2] and there can be little doubt that the majority of these are paid according to the various systems known generically as 'piecework'. Put at its most simple, piecework pays the worker according to the number of items that he produces; that is, it relates all or a part of the money he gets to the level of his output by direct linear proportion.

Although payment is normally related to a worker's output, piecework is primarily intended to reward labour input. Labour input may be crudely characterized by the combination of a measure of time with some measure of the effort maintained by the worker over that time. The great imponderable is the measurement of effort. For not only does the nature of effort vary from job to job; it also varies from person to person. Effort is a subjective experience. However, with some bold assumptions about one worker being roughly substitutable for another, this problem can be circumvented.

WORK STUDY

The core of work study is the technique known as 'effort rating'. This is based upon the concept of the 'standard effort'. The standard effort is the level of effort which a normal, qualified operator who is working under an incentive can maintain on any job over a period of time. It provides the datum line for effort rating. It is the contention of trained work study engineers that they can identify the standard level of effort for jobs which are qualitatively very different. Further, it is contended that they can 'rate' levels of effort above and below the standard according to a linear scale. The scale is geared to a certain index for a

---

Incentive Payment Systems, London: Staples, 1957, provides a general analysis of different types of system. L. Klein, *Multiproducts Ltd*, London: HMSO, 1964, provides a detailed study of the organizational characteristics of a piecework system.

[2] Estimate given by the Engineering Employers' Federation for its own membership. See NBPI *op. cit.*

standard effort (sometimes this is 100 points) with a theoretical minimum of zero.

In closely controlled piecework systems the job of the work study engineer is rigorous and highly formalized. He first watches a normal, trained operator work at the job and checks that the method used is the best possible. He breaks complete 'cycles' of the operation into short 'elements', notes the time that each takes, and the level of effort which the operator puts forth. After timing a large number of cycles, and rating the effort exerted during each, he calculates the 'standard time' (that is, the time it would take at a standard effort) that is implied by his results for each element of each cycle. Depending upon the type of system in use, for each element he calculates the modal, average or median standard time from the results of the many cycles. During his study he will have recorded the amount of time lost because of interruptions and will estimate how much time should be allowed for such contingencies. He then adds a fixed percentage allowance for personal needs to the sum of the element times, including the contingency allowances. This produces the final standard time for the job.[3]

This procedure provides an inductive and systematic method of making useful predictions about future behaviour. It provides an estimate of the number of pieces per hour the average experienced worker will produce. The result of the work study may be used for accounting or technical purposes quite unrelated to the value-laden problem of payment, such as the measurement of total labour content for a job or to co-ordinate work stations on a production flow-line. For such purposes there is no practical alternative measure of labour content.

Of course such procedures cannot eliminate the subjective element in effort rating. Variations in judgements of effort are too large to be respectable by normal scientific

[3] For a discussion of the literature on the precision of work study techniques, see N. A. Dudley, *Work Measurement: Some Research Studies*, London: Macmillan, 1968.

principles. Rigorous procedures may help the work study engineer to achieve more consistent standards, but, at heart, effort rating is an intuitive process in which the work study engineer draws upon his past experience.[4]

Work study has been criticized because work study engineers from different workplaces exhibit different standards.[5] But, as Behrend observes,[6] work study need not achieve universally applicable standards to justify itself; it need only provide consistent standards within individual establishments or other areas of common reference.

Two refinements of work study deserve mention. The first is the techniques called 'pre-determined motion-time systems' which go under a number of trade names. These provide standard time data for a large number of very simple body movements such as reaching out, closing one's grasp, bending a wrist and so on. In principle it is possible to build up standard times for any jobs from these data. It is usually accepted, however, that they require some adjustment from one factory to another. A more common refinement is the use of 'synthetic' standard times which

[4] 'The true purpose of scientific objectivity in the practice of work measurement is precisely the opposite of what it claims to be in theory: though precision and consistency in the form of technical terms and measuring appliances are indispensible, and even important, they have the function, not of eliminating the intrusion of effort conceptions, *but, on the contrary,* of detecting and making them all the more amenable to consistent guesswork.' W. Baldamus, *Efficiency and Effort,* London: Tavistock, 1961, p. 45.

[5] Such results are quoted in T. Lupton, *Money for Effort,* London: HMSO, 1961, and N. A. Dudley, *op. cit.*

[6] H. Behrend, 'A Fair Day's Work', *Scottish Journal of Political Economy,* June 1961. An important concept that has been developed in this context is that of the 'effort bargain', that is the trade-off between wages and effort through 'the interlocking of standardised effort and wage expectations' (W. Baldamus, 'The Relationship between Wage and Effort', *Journal of Industrial Economics,* 1957). Much depends upon how sensitive individuals are to their effort bargains. Unfortunately, the subjective nature of effort makes the concept inherently resistant to empirical study. It has thus proved difficult to assess the importance of the effort bargain as an explanation of variations in wages and effort between different work situations. See Baldamus, JIE, *op. cit.*, and H. Behrend, 'The Effort Bargain', *Industrial and Labor Relations Review,* 1957.

are built up within an establishment. When a new job is to be timed, the work study engineer ascertains whether it has elements which are identical to elements of past jobs for which he has already determined standard times. These elements are called 'synthetic elements' and, with a large library of synthetics, work study engineers frequently are able to calculate all or most of a new standard time without touching a stop watch.

Many piecework systems are less rigorous than those described here.[7] In some, generally known as 'ratefixed' systems, no systematic attempt is made to rate effort and sometimes no stop watches are used. The ratefixers use the same intuitive faculty as work study engineers but they lack the discipline of the procedure and of careful timing. Standards set by ratefixers are probably less accurate and less insulated from bargaining pressures. This is particularly serious where cycles are measured in minutes and seconds because small errors can give rise to gross anomalies. When jobs take several hours, days or even weeks per cycle, this inaccuracy of ratefixing is less significant.

THE INCORPORATION OF THE MONEY RATE

The techniques that have been described permit the work content of jobs to be expressed in terms of standard times. By introducing a money rate per hour, output can be expressed in terms of earnings. For example, if the standard time for a job is expressed as 'x minutes per piece' or, alternatively, as '$\frac{60}{x}$ pieces per hour', and if the 'base rate' of payment is 'r pence per hour', then the bonus earnings of an operator who works at ten per cent above standard effort and produces $\frac{66}{x}$ pieces per hour will be 1.1r pence per hour.

Some piecework systems put a money 'price' to each

[7] It has been noted that engineering factories with piecework systems make much greater use of work study in Glasgow than in Birmingham. D. I. MacKay, D. Boddy, J. Brack, J. A. Diack, N. Jones, *Labour Markets under Different Employment Conditions*, London: Allen and Unwin, 1971, p. 106.

operation by simply relating the standard time to the money base rate. Thus a base rate of 'r pence per hour' would give a price of '$\frac{xr}{60}$ pence per piece'. The relative merits of valuing piecework operations with standard times as opposed to with standard prices are often debated. An argument commonly heard among work study engineers is that standard prices are the more vulnerable to bargaining pressures. The case studies, however, showed that systems using standard times can become the subject of bargaining just as much as those using standard prices.

One species of piecework analytically distinct from those described is that which employs no base rate at all; the operations are priced simply as 'y pence per piece'. Historically this is the oldest form of piecework and it is still operated by some major firms. It might be termed 'primitive ratefixing'. Such a system gives the ratefixer wide discretion. Unlike his counterparts in establishments with piecework base rates he has an explicit commitment to relate piecework values to an expected level of earnings. On being given a new operation to ratefix he asks himself, in effect: 'Given that the prevailing norm in this factory at the moment is for a worker who works at a standard effort to earn n pence per hour, what price should I put on this operation in order that a standard effort on it will yield n pence?' His procedure will in fact be very similar to that of other ratefixers. He will use the same process of observation and intuition to size up the operation and to estimate the time it will take under a standard effort. Instead of stating the time or of multiplying it by the base rate to yield a standard price, he calculates the price he must give for that operation in order that it will provide the expected level of hourly earnings for a standard effort.

A term that is commonly used for 'standard time' by ratefixers is that of 'floor-to-floor time'. Both refer to the time within which a normal qualified operator, working under an incentive, might be expected to complete the operation. In this study the term piecework 'value' will be used loosely to include standard times, floor-to-floor times, and standard prices, as well as the 'allowed times and prices discussed later. Changing terminologies appear to be an occupational hazard of those concerned with piecework systems, technical terms being cast aside when they become sullied with bargaining associations.

Bonus earnings alone do not usually provide the whole wage. Apart from any overtime that may be worked, most piecework systems provide the worker with a proportion of his wage that does not vary with output. The composition of a pieceworker's wage differs considerably from one establishment to another. Even those firms which are members of the Engineering Employers' Federation often have little in common in this respect, the national negotiations having only the effect of increasing the fixed part of the wage.[8]

THE RELEVANCE OF NATIONAL AGREEMENTS

The piecework systems of federated engineering firms operate against a background of national agreements and these might be expected to influence the conduct of bargaining. A detailed discussion of these agreements is to be found in Marsh's study[9] where it is emphasized that they have always done no more than provide a background to those agreements already established within the plants. Two provisions are important in this context.

[8] Since the War the nationally negotiated wage increases have contributed to a rate called the Piecework Supplement (PWS) for pieceworkers and to the Consolidated Time Rate (CTR) for time-rate workers. The CTR is also the basis for overtime payment for pieceworkers. For the purpose of negotiation there is a Piecework Base Rate (PWBR). The national agreements used to lay down a Minimum Piecework Standard (MPWS) such that an operator of 'average ability' should earn $\text{MPWS} = (\text{PWS} + 1 \cdot 45 \times \text{PWBR})$. The 1964 Package Deal agreement altered this pattern. From 1968 the CTR was increased and renamed the Minimum Time Rate (MTR). In order to maintain the old equivalence, the PWBR was increased with the effect that the new $\text{MPWS} = (1 \cdot 15 \times \text{MTR})$. All these rates have a number of money values for different skill levels.

[9] A. Marsh, *Industrial Relations in Engineering*, London: Pergamon, 1965.

The first is the so-called 'mutuality clause'. One formulation[10] states:

> The price to be paid or basis time to be allowed either for a new job or for an altered job shall be fixed by mutual arrangement between the employer and the work-man who is to perform the work or by such methods as now exist or may hereafter be established by agreement in any trade or district.

This can be interpreted in several ways. Some would see it as a deliberate attempt to exclude trade unions from the agreement of piecework job values which, once agreed by one worker, become binding on all. Others see it to be important in forcing management to come to an agreement with workers on all values rather than being able to dictate them.

The second important feature of the national agreements is clauses which lay down that[11]

> No piecework price, bonus or basis time once fixed may be altered unless the material, means or method of production is changed.... When the material, means or method of production is changed and the employer desires a modification in price or basis time, the modification shall in no case be such as to effect a reduction in the earnings of the worker concerned.

The significance of this provision will be discussed in the next section.

The true status of these agreements today is not at all obvious. At most, they only augment existing plant agreements and 'custom and practice' rules and, as will be established in a subsequent chapter, the rules governing piece-

[10] Agreement between Engineering Employers' Federation and National Federation of General Workers, 6th April 1920.

[11] *ibid.* As Marsh (op. cit, 167-9) describes, the piecework agreements with the individual unions differ in small but important particulars and several major engineering unions (notably the AUEW) have no comprehensive piecework agreements with the EEF. The details of these variations do not affect this general discussion.

work bargaining in practice not only differ from those in national agreements, they also differ from plant to plant. The importance of the two provisions quoted lies not so much in the fact that they have influenced the rules actually prevailing in factories today (whether or not this is the case is an historical imponderable) as in the undoubted fact that, in broad spirit, they represent the generally prevailing rules on these sensitive areas of the piecework bargain in most establishments. It is likely that in most factories with other than wholly docile workforces, these two rules of 'mutuality' and 'material, means or method' will apply and the national agreements make them minimum provisions to which workers can appeal in disputes. It will be demonstrated later that, under certain conditions, the prevailing rules can become very much more generous to workers than these.

The Sources of Instability

Techniques of ratefixing and work study are designed to provide establishments with piecework systems that are internally consistent. For a system to be considered objective and fair it is necessary for workers to believe that equal effort is rewarded with equal pay. Problems arise when anomalous piecework values generate levels of earnings which affront workers' sense of 'fairness'. When this happens the legitimacy of the method of determining piecework values may be questioned and contested. As workers then begin to introduce new criteria for valuing jobs, the system becomes open to bargaining pressures. The argument of this section is that, with the passage of time, all piecework systems are liable to experience such anomalies.

AUTONOMOUS' MECHANISMS OF DISRUPTION

The most obvious cause of anomalous piecework values is that of error on the part of the work study engineer or ratefixer. Even the most accomplished work study engineers do not claim to be within more than 95 per cent of accurate

Or always was. "The System" is not rigid; equilibrium is a varying and dynamic concept.
∴ "anomalies", which derive from 1215 view, is wrong

standards. Operators may be able to confuse them during their work. If an error should arise that produces a piecework value that is too 'tight' (that is, yielding relatively low earnings for a given effort), the operator is likely to appeal against it and get it rectified. If, on the other hand, the resultant value is too 'slack', in all but the most passive of workforces management will be unable to correct it once it has been accepted and worked with; it will have become established under the principles of 'custom and practice'. Work study engineers and ratefixers become haunted by the irrevocable results of their past errors.

A second source of incorrect piecework values is that of technical innovation and alteration. Often these problems arise as a result of poor communications between the work study engineers or ratefixers on the one hand and the production engineers and their equivalents on the other. If a machine or method is altered and if as a result operator earnings improve, the work study engineers or ratefixers may not discover this until it is too late to adjust the piecework values concerned.

While management can take steps to improve its internal communications there are other more intangible forms of technical alteration that disturb piecework values. These are gradual improvements in materials and techniques, sometimes remote in origin from the operation affected. The case studies showed that improvements in plant layout and organization could have significant effects. Improvements in the technical specifications of unprocessed components could make subsequent operations shorter. An instance of change that affected many of the factories studied was the improvement over the last decade in the quality and type of machine-tool cutting-tip. Even the most zealous of work study engineers would find it impossible to compensate for such elusive developments despite their long-term importance.

A third source of anomalies comes with the phenomenon of the 'learning curve'. This is a general term for the well-recorded[12] fact that, on all but the most unskilled of jobs, operators tend to improve their performance with the passage of time and the accumulation of experience. On some operations this improvement can continue for several years. In only two of the factories studied were determined attempts made to accommodate and neutralize the effect of this learning curve on earnings. This was done by compensating the earnings of the operator involved for a certain period (its duration depending upon the nature of the job) until he had grown familiar with it. Even the most careful of efforts by management in these factories did not succeed in eliminating the effect of the learning curve in producing abnormally high earnings.

It might be argued that learning curve improvements in earnings would not be classed as anomalous by the work force. If such an improvement comes from increased skill then it is acceptable under the notion of the effort bargain. But even if this is accepted as valid in the short-run, in the longer-run, as operators move from job to job, the argument breaks down. It has already been mentioned that some national agreements provide that an operator's earnings should not suffer as a result of an alteration of a piecework value. An extension of this, whose exact application varies between establishments, is the 'custom and practice' rule that a worker's earnings should not suffer as a result of a transfer to a different job. If either or both of these rules hold in a piecework system it is not difficult to see that when operators experience changes in jobs with learning curve properties, then earnings are liable to rise in a way that is inconsistent with any theoretical effort bargain. As an instance, an operator might start work on a job 'A' and, after initially earning bonus at a level 'b', will gradually improve his performance so that he is earning, say, 'b + p'. When he is moved to job 'B' he will be able to appeal to 'custom and practice' so that he starts that job with a piecework value that will yield him earnings of 'b +

[12] NBPI *op. cit.,* Supplement, Paper 3.

p' from the start. Although he may carry some of his 'learning' over from his previous job, it is likely that, once again his performance will improve with time and, by the time he is moved to job 'C' his earnings may have reached 'b + p + q' for no greater level of effort or skill than when he was working on 'A' for 'b + p'. The process will continue indefinitely. Clearly the rate of increase of earnings that result will depend upon the shape of the individual learning curves, upon the frequency of the changes, upon the prevailing 'custom and practice' rules, and upon the ability of the work study engineers and ratefixers to compensate for the learning effect.

It can be seen that the combination of these technical shortcomings of work study and of the 'ratchet' mechanisms which prevent their being rectified, produce powerful mechanisms whereby anomalous piecework values are created with the passage of time. In common with the NBPI Payment by Results Report[13] we can refer to them as 'autonomous mechanisms'. Their distinguishing feature is that they are not the product of direct bargaining pressures.

Two points should be made about the autonomous mechanisms. The first is that they all lead to an increase in unit labour costs above what they would otherwise be; that is, they are all inflationary. Increases in earnings that arise from the learning curve are only covered by increasing labour productivity in the first instance; the ratcheting of earnings that occurs with subsequent job changes increases unit costs. The increases in earnings that arise from exogenous technical change in piecework systems usually have nothing to do with the piecework system *per se* but come as 'windfalls' to workers for no increase in effort on their part.

The second point arises from this. Because increases in earnings from autonomous mechanisms come as chance windfalls to those workers favoured by them, they have little

[13] NBPI *op. cit.*

chance of being seen to be 'fair' under the notion of the effort bargain. Consequently they are liable to create feelings of injustice among other workers and hence are liable to disrupt the piecework system in which they grow.

That all piecework systems are subject to autonomous forces of disruption is suggested by more than the description of the commonplace technical features already given. A case study described in the NBPI Payment by Results Report Supplement[14] provides strong factual evidence. Here, in conditions of management control that were close to ideal and with no significant bargaining pressure on the part of operators, the case study worker found an exceptional quantity of statistical data about a product assembly line that had remained unchanged for five years. Even here, however, the scatter of earnings had widened and average earnings had risen. Over that period the increase in earnings was at an annual average compound rate of 1.8 per cent even when all formally negotiated wage increases were excluded. When improvements in productivity were taken into account, there was still an annual rate of increase of earnings of about 1 per cent. These increases must have been largely the result of autonomous mechanisms.

THE DEVELOPMENT OF BARGAINING PRESSURES

As anomalous earnings emerge through these autonomous mechanisms, the scatter of individual earnings tends to increase and the connection between pay and effort becomes weakened. The weakening of this relationship is liable to influence the attitude of pieceworkers towards the legitimacy of the formal process of determining piecework values. Just how far they challenge their work study engineers depends very much upon the bargaining climate of the factory—a subject to which the discussion will return in a later chapter. In some factories gross anomalies in pay were passively tolerated as being matters of good and bad luck over which workers had no control. In others, to differing extents,

[14] *ibid.*, Supplement, Paper 6.

anomalies could become objects of strife and coercive comparison and the whole process of fixing piecework values tended to become a bargaining matter.

The emergence of bargaining pressures in competition with formal work study as determinants of piecework values does not by any means remove *all* sense of legitimacy from the procedures of the work study engineers and ratefixers. Divergent and even conflicting criteria appear to coexist quite easily in piecework systems. The case studies showed a range of experience between factories from an unquestioned acceptance of work study at one end to a wholly bargained system with no pretence at scientific method at the other. In between, work study was sometimes the dominant factor in fixing values with minor bargaining occurring in difficult situations and with argumentative operators. Sometimes work study engineers and ratefixers did not pretend that their measuring procedure was intended to do more than give them a basis from which they could bargain adequately. At some factories they admitted that their procedure was no more than an empty ritual to give a professional veneer to a hard bargain carried out under the threat of sanctions.

Once bargaining over piecework values has become widespread within a factory, anomalies begin to arise for reasons other than autonomous mechanisms. 'Secondary drift' of piecework values develops as pieceworkers attempt to restore the differentials that the autonomous mechanisms have disrupted. In time, the autonomous mechanisms become relatively insignificant. As will be discussed in detail in Chapter Three, the main force behind the bargaining process becomes one of comparison in an unending stream of fragmented bargains between individual workers and junior managers. As the NBPI Report observed, 'once a PBR system gets out of effective management control, it takes on a life of its own as individuals and groups seize on any chance of raising their earnings to the level that they think is fair'.[15]

How the System Adjusts to Bargaining

The normal pattern of work in an average engineering piecework factory demands many thousand piecework values to be in existence at any one time. As new jobs come in and as specifications and techniques alter so fresh values must be introduced. At any one moment the piecework values that men are working with will come from many different 'vintages': some will have been agreed upon in the last month; others will have remained unchanged for many years. The work study engineers and ratefixers are essentially doing no more than servicing and maintaining a massive and slowly changing accumulation of agreements.

Once piecework systems become distorted there is a tendency for conceptions as to what is a fair wage to drift upwards. Even without explicit bargaining pressures it becomes extremely difficult for work study engineers and ratefixers to obtain an operator's agreement upon a fresh, and strictly accurate, standard piecework value. Both management and the operator can see that, by comparison with the earnings that the general run of established piecework values are yielding, the earnings on this new standard value will simply not be 'fair'.

On meeting this problem the question that management has to face is how individual piecework values might be 'slackened' without disturbing the whole edifice. In the factories with quiescent work forces the work study engineers are able to add on 'special allowances' to any piecework times which they see would (if they were determined strictly) be found excessively 'tight' by comparison with those on neighbouring jobs. This selective treatment is used very sparingly and it is apparently not understood by the operators concerned. But in factories whose workforces have greater

[15] NBPI *op. cit.*

collective awareness, this sort of selective treatment is unlikely to be permitted. It is liable to be 'universalized' as a precedent for 'custom and practice' and the use of special allowances would be bargained for by all.

Nor is it effective to raise piecework base rates. This would raise all earnings without either narrowing their dispersion or improving the relative position of those with the 'tightest' and newest piecework values. It is common for firms not to have increased their piecework base rates for many years, in some cases for two decades or more.

What actually happens is that the work study engineers and ratefixers reach agreement with individual piece-workers in such a way that job values become progressively 'slacker' than the strict standard values. These job values are commonly distinguished from standards by being called 'allowed' values. With the passage of time, average earnings drift upwards under autonomous and possibly under bargaining pressures. Consequently the gap widens between the standard value applicable to any new job, and the allowed value which is actually agreed for it. The percentage by which the allowed value differs from the appropriate standard value is commonly called the 'conversion factor.'

THE 'CONVERSION FACTOR'

Like many another institution that has evolved rather than been designed, conversion factors tend to be surrounded by considerable mystification. Usually there is no explicit policy whereby successive vintages of piecework values come to be 'converted' at increasing percentages. Work study engineers and ratefixers do it tacitly because, by gradually raising the floor on which piecework earnings rest, they increase the likelihood of prompt agreement on new allowed values.

The amount of control that management has over the conversion factor is an important determinant of the amount of control it can maintain over the piecework system as a whole. At one extreme an example can be given of a factory where the conversion factor was used as a positive instrument of control by management. Here there was little doubt that the relatively passive workforce did not understand the complex piecework system. The management made great use of work study for accounting and production control purposes and the same standard times were used for these as for the piecework system. It was consequently felt to be vital to prevent their distortion by bargaining pressures. The use of 'special allowances' already mentioned helped to shelter anomalies but it was still necessary to use a conversion factor. Over the thirty years that the piecework system had been in operation this factor had been periodically increased by steps so that, at the time of the study, allowed times were about three times as large as their respective standard times. The conversion factor was explicit and rigorously adhered to. When, every few years, it was increased, piecework allowed times fixed thenceforth would start from a new and increased base and, because new times would otherwise tend to yield relatively low earnings, the scatter of earnings would be prevented from becoming too large. Here there could be no doubt that the conversion factor was a vital tool in the control of the piecework system. Without it either the basic standards would have become too distorted to be of use to other management functions or the piecework system would have become so manifestly unfair that even this factory's passive workforce would have questioned its legitimacy.

The other cases were not so clear-cut. Another factory with notably quiescent workers had an orderly piecework system. It achieved this not by an explicit conversion factor but by the work study engineers' permitting their effort rating standards very gradually to slip. Their effort rating scales that once rated a standard effort at 80 points were found to have gradually shifted (under the approving care of the chief work study engineer) so that at the time of the case study they were rating a standard effort at about 110 points. This implicit use of a conversion factor meant that the work study engineers dealt only in allowed times.

But it meant there were no standard times which production engineers and the like could make use of.

The position of the conversion factor becomes much more indeterminate where bargaining pressures are stronger. One such factory had a jointly negotiated factor which was periodically increased. This undoubtedly helped control the pay system but it tended to throw the burden of the bargaining back onto floor-to-floor times and contingency allowances. Under very heavy bargaining the conversion factor may cease to have any independent significance. In one plant the foremen (who played a large part in the bargain) said that 'officially' the conversion factor was 200 per cent but that they in practice worked on the assumption that it was 400 to 500 per cent. The shop stewards, on the other hand, said that 600 per cent was the factor upon which they expected workers to reach agreement on allowed values.

Pulled by the remorseless forces of piecework wage drift and tied down to fixed base rates, piecework systems tend to distort in idiosyncratic ways. An example is provided by a factory which originally operated a relatively sophisticated piecework system based upon work study. Bargaining pressures caused the work study engineers' effort rating standards to drift downwards and caused contingency allowances to become artificially inflated. More serious injury was done to the system when senior management (against the advice of the work study engineers) reached agreements with the shop stewards that explicitly mentioned the level of earnings that a 'normal' worker should be able to achieve. This had the double result of forcing the work study engineers to devise inflated base rates and of exposing their slipped work study standards, both of which (for rather esoteric reasons) further weakened their methods. The result at the time of the case study was a piecework system with no stated conversion factor but a collection of rules of thumb whereby the work study engineers could use the formal language of their profession to cobble together piecework values acceptable to the workers. Apart from the jargon used, their job differed little from that of 'primitive ratefixers'.

A report of a study group of managers of the Coventry and District Engineering Employers' Association concerned with the control of piecework systems came to the conclusion that the introduction of conversion factors could be valuable in disciplining the bargaining process.[16] The importance of an explicit conversion factor lies fundamentally in the opportunity it provides for distinguishing between the two distinct issues with which piecework bargaining concerns itself: the floor-to-floor times and the desired earnings. These will be discussed later.

The Theoretical Enigma

Once the official means of determining job values has collapsed under the pressure of heavy bargaining, the entire piecework system tends to be taken over by extremely fragmented bargaining between individual workers (or possibly gangs of them) and ratefixers (or work study engineers or foremen). Joint negotiation over piecework base rates ceases. Even the role of the shop steward is subsidiary; he tends only to be called in to mediate in the more intractable of individual bargains. The question raised by this is whether the process can be considered as collective bargaining in any sense.

Flanders draws a sharp distinction between the individual bargain between a worker and his employer on the one hand and the misleadingly named 'collective bargain' between groups of workers and an employer (or employers) on the other. The individual bargain

provides for an exchange of work for wages and, in stipulating the conditions of the exchange, adjusts for the time being conflicts of interest between a buyer and a seller of

[16] Coventry and District Engineering Employers' Association, *Wage Drift, Work Measurement and Systems of Payment,* Coventry, 1967. This remains the most realistic discussion of piecework from a management point of view.

labour. A collective agreement, on the other hand, though it is frequently called a collective bargain and in some countries where it has legal force a collective contract, does not commit anyone to buy or sell labour. It does something quite different. It is meant to ensure that when labour is bought and sold (the specific kinds of labour referred to) its price and the other terms of the transaction will accord with the provisions of the agreement. These provisions are in fact a body of rules intended to regulate among other things the terms of employment contracts. Thus collective bargaining is itself essentially a rule-making process, and this is a feature which has no proper counterpart in individual bargaining.[17]

He observes that collective bargaining regulates rather than replaces individual bargaining. Collective bargaining is a 'pressure group' activity and

the resulting deals, though they may be called 'bargains', are in reality compromise settlements of power conflicts. This brings us to the second truly characteristic feature of collective bargaining, apart from its being a rule-making process, namely that it is 'a power relationship between organisations'. Accordingly the process of negotiation is best described as a diplomatic use of power.

The distinction is, at heart, one between an economic and a political process.

The immediate question raised by Flanders' analysis is whether the fragmented bargaining that occurs under piecework can be considered to be equivalent to the 'individual bargaining' described by him. Does the pieceworker battling it out with the ratefixer approximate to an economic man? If this were the case one would expect earnings movements under piecework bargaining to be sensitive to the state of the labour market. The next chapter explores this relationship. Since it finds that, with qualifications, it is weak and that the average pieceworker is far from a puppet to market forces, Chapter Three studies the dynamics of piecework

[17] A. Flanders, 'Collective Bargaining: A Theoretical Analysis', in *Management and Unions*, London: Faber, 1970, pp. 216–9.

earnings within the plant in search of other determinants of wage movements.

The second question raised by Flanders' analysis arises from the observation that collective bargaining combines the exercise of power with the formation and administration of rules. In any political system, rules (whether they are laws, agreements, conventions or anything else) are important because they bring at least temporary stability to a situation of conflicting interest groups. Although piecework systems are often written off as 'anarchic', this is far from the truth. As Chapter Four will establish, they are in fact regulated by complex structures of rules. These rules are understood by those who work with them and they are established against the ever-visible background of a power relationship. And yet, and herein lies the central enigma, these rules have never been negotiated.

Negotiation, the 'diplomatic use of power', has two distinguishing characteristics. The first is that it is conducted by representatives whose position is in some way legitimized (by either election or appointment) by those whom they represent. The second is that it is a deliberate process with the representatives acting intentionally. The enigma is that fresh rules and wage increases emerge through collective bargaining processes which are, to use an ungainly term, 'non-negotiated'. Why should the representatives permit this situation to arise? Chapter Five considers this question for the stewards and Chapter Six for management.

If this study can be said to have one major purpose, it is the analysis of the non-negotiated processes of collective bargaining. Their importance both to the regulation of piecework bargaining and also to piecework wage determination will, it is hoped, be made clear. But it will also be argued that they are fundamental to an understanding of what the Donovan Commission called informal workplace bargaining. Thus the analysis should have a relevance beyond the confines of piecework payment systems.

2

The Conventional Economic Determinants

Any analysis of wage bargaining finds that explanations involving the exercise of power are closely interwoven with those involving the competitive forces of the labour market. These deal in different sorts of causation. It is consequently important to distinguish between them and to map out where the usefulness of one gives way to the usefulness of the other.

At the end of the last chapter it was stressed that collective bargaining was best understood as a political activity, not in the sense of party or state politics, but as an activity in which conflicting pressure groups come to temporary accommodation through the agreement of rules. But the question was also raised that the very fragmented bargaining that occurs under piecework may be exceptionally susceptible to economic influence. There are two economic factors which deserve particular attention. The first is the extent to which the pressure of demand in the labour market influences the outcome of the piecework bargain. The second is the importance of exogenous increases in labour productivity in increasing earnings quite separately from any bargaining. It is first necessary, however, to clarify the definition of the earnings whose movements are the centre of attention.

The Notion of 'Wage Drift'

All definitions of wage drift contain, implicitly or otherwise, a political assumption about the level at which pay 'ought', in some sense, to be determined. Phelps Brown's definition refers to 'a rise in the effective rate of pay per unit of labour input that is brought about by arrangements outside the control of the recognized procedures for scheduling wage rates.'[1] For a long time there were good institutional reasons—and even better statistical ones—for treating national negotiations as the 'recognized procedures'. But during the 1960s this became increasingly unsatisfactory. Especially in the private sector of the economy, national negotiations accounted for less and less of annual wage increases and, for some industries, they deliberately changed to fixing no more than minimum wages. At the same time there was growing pressure to formalize wage bargaining at plant and company level. The Donovan Commission saw this as unavoidable and desirable and the Industrial Relations Act is likely to hasten the change.

However, even if the distinction between national negotiations and other 'arrangements' for determining wages has diminished in utility, concern with incomes policies has sharpened interest in wage drift. But the area where this interest is concentrated is that of bargaining below national level. Statistical information about this area is hard to come by and institutional information is difficult to generalize. As a result, the notion of wage drift has, on the established definition, become largely inoperational and useless and it is necessary for this study to define it more precisely.

The revised definition is based upon the distinction drawn at the end of the last chapter between 'negotiated' and 'non-negotiated' processes. Although both are aspects of collective bargaining, the distinguishing feature of negotiation is that it is an intentional activity carried out between representatives whose role is legitimized by those whom they represent. The nature of non-negotiated rules will be discussed in Chapter Four; here the concern is purely with wages. Some wage increases arise from explicit

[1] E. H. Phelps-Brown, 'Wage Drift', *Economica,* 1962.

negotiations between managers and shop stewards at plant or company level and are in the form of generally applicable rates. Examples of these negotiated increases are additions to timerates, piecework base rates, shift allowances, measured daywork rates and the like. Other increases come from individual bargains over individual rates or job values. These are 'non-negotiated' increases and their most obvious source is fragmented piecework bargaining. They also arise from the fiddles, windfalls and increases in productivity of individual pieceworkers, from bargaining over merit rates and condition money and the like and, in certain circumstances, from bargaining over 'institutionalized' overtime.

The make-up (or 'composition') of an individual's wage is the accretion of past wage increases and reflects both the level and the manner of settlement. Here it will be considered in three components. First there is the nationally negotiated component (N) which for pieceworkers will be taken as the Minimum Piecework Standard.[2] Second, there are the various additions negotiated at plant or company level (F) which, in a piecework wage, may be additions to the base rate, to the fixed component, or 'policy' additions to the conversion factor. Third and finally, there are the non-negotiated additions (G) defined as the percentage of earnings (excluding overtime) that has arisen without explicit negotiations between representatives over generally applicable money rates. These last two components (F+G) are together variously termed 'workplace margin', 'earnings gap' and 'wage gap'. They may merge into one another to some extent, and, as Chapter Five will discuss, their ultimate definition requires a judgement about the political

[2] This is also used by S. W. Lerner and J. Marquand, 'Workshop Bargaining, Wage Drift and Productivity in the British Engineering Industry', *Manchester School of Economic and Social Studies*, January 1960, and by P. J. Sloane, 'Wage Drift: with reference to case studies in the engineering industry of Central Scotland', *Journal of Economic Studies*, 1967. After 1968 it is necessary to increase the Minimum Piecework Standard prevailing before that time by subsequent increases in the Piecework Supplement.

processes at the workplace but for the current discussion of piecework the distinction is fairly robust.

The National Board for Prices and Incomes measured drift as 'the actual increase in the "workplace margin" as a proportion of total earnings... excluding overtime'.[3] In the symbols given here this is

$$\frac{(F+G)_{(t)} - (F+G)_{(t-1)}}{(N+F+G)_{(t-1)}} \times 100$$

as a percentage rate of change. In a similar way, for this study the rate of non-negotiated wage drift will be defined as

$$\frac{G_{(t)} - G_{(t-1)}}{(N+F+G)_{(t-1)}} \times 100$$

although for some of the statistical analyses a slightly different measure is used.

A further measure indicates the relative importance of non-negotiated wage determination processes. This may be defined as the percentage of the increase in standard earnings that arises from non-negotiated drift and put in symbolic terms (measured over a period of n years) as

$$\frac{G_{(t+n)} - G_{(t)}}{(N+F+G)_{(t+n)} - (N+F+G)_{(t)}} \times 100$$

This measure will be used extensively later in the analysis when it becomes important to consider how far the wage determination processes of a factory are beyond the reach of negotiations. Consequently, it will be called the 'Topsy factor' since it is to Topsy[4] that a wide range of managers and unionists habitually refer when asked how an evolved institution came into being. 'It wasn't ever designed or planned', they say, 'it just "grow'd".'

THE SIGNIFICANCE OF TOPSY

This division of the wage into three components N, F and G has nothing necessarily to do with its division into

---

[3] NBPI *op. cit.*
[4] 'Do you know who made you?'
'Nobody, as I knows on,' said the child with a short laugh ...
'I s'pect I grow'd. Don't think nobody never made me.'
from *Uncle Tom's Cabin* by Harriet Beecher Stowe.

fixed and variable components—that will receive attention
in the next chapter. The three-fold division is a 'small-p
political' one indicating the bargaining origins of the wage.
The Topsy factor is an indicator of the extent to which
piecework wage increases in a period arise outside formal
negotiating processes at either national or local level.

Table 2:1 presents data to cast further light upon this
categorization. It shows for each of the ten factories covered
in this study the origins of the increases in standard piecework wages over periods of several years. It also shows the
average annual compound rate of non-negotiated wage
drift for each factory for the same period. The figures
should be treated with caution because many statistical
problems arose in their compilation, not the least being the
different periods over which wage data were available. The
annual rate figures should not be taken as accurate to more
than half a per cent, but, given a margin of error, there is
no reason to suppose them misleading for the purpose of
this study.

Factory E in the Table has had no nationally negotiated
increases because it is not a member of the Engineering
Employers' Federation and does not follow their agreements. All the other factories received approximately the
same amount from national awards (making allowance for
the different time periods). Because the absolute level of
earnings varies between factories, the proportion of their
increase in earnings coming from the national awards varies
also. It is not fruitful to consider the absolute levels of earnings as such because the factories differ in labour market
and skill mix. Generally, however, (as can be deduced from
the Table) there is a close relationship between the level of
absolute earnings and the size of the Topsy factor. The
higher a factory's piecework earnings are relative to others
in the same labour market, the higher one can expect its
Topsy factor to be. Putting this another way, it is possible
to generalize that factories whose piecework earnings are
low relative to their neighbours' make greater use of formal
plant or company level negotiations. This relationship was

TABLE 2:1

The sources of increases in standard piecework earnings by factory

The percentage of the overall increase over a period contributed by non-negotiated drift, negotiated drift and national negotiations.

THE BARGAINING ORIGINS OF THE INCREASE	*FACTORY* A	*B*	*C*	*D*	*E*	*F*	*G*	*H*	*J*	*K*
TOPSY FACTOR: the percentage of increase arising from NON-NEGOTIATED drift	83	78	81	57	66	77	81	20	45	35
the percentage of increase arising from NEGOTIATED drift at plant or company	—	—	—	23	34	—	—	37	14	13
the percentage of increase NEGOTIATED NATIONALLY	17	22	19	20	—	23	19	43	41	52
average annual compound increase in standard earnings arising from non-negotiated drift	5·0	4·8	5·1	3·1	4·5	5·0	6·5	1·8	2·1	1·2
time period of measurement	1963–9	1963–9	1963–9	1965–9	1966–9	1963–9	1963–7	1961–7	1961–7	1963–7

checked by selecting a sample of six firms in Coventry and estimating their Topsy factors specifically for skilled piece-workers; the higher the firms were on the 'league table' of average earnings, the greater were their Topsy factors. Although there is room for a more thorough testing of the relationship, it appears to be quite strong.

The hypothesis upon which the significance of the Topsy factor rests is that non-negotiated drift is inherently more inflationary than negotiated drift. It appears to be the case that, for pieceworkers, formal plant-level negotiations are generally a last resort when non-negotiated drift fails to deliver the goods. The 'goods' here might be defined in terms of the maintenance of accepted differentials both with-in and between plants. In addition, the hypothesis implies that non-negotiated drift is not just a passive response to widening differentials but that non-negotiated bargaining processes have an inherent 'bootstrap' property of generat-ing earnings increases of their own accord. An explanation of this process must wait till Chapter Six after piecework bargaining has been analysed in greater detail.

This tentative hypothesis can be illustrated by the examples of three Coventry firms. The first had never had any formal plant negotiations for skilled pieceworkers and, under heavy piecework bargaining, average earnings gradu-ally moved up the league table of earnings of factories in the city. This plant had a high Topsy factor. A second factory had a history of paternalistic management and of very little bargaining activity. Consequently it experienced almost no non-negotiated drift and its average earnings would periodically fall away from average earnings in the city. When management felt that the gap had got too wide they would initiate formal plant-level negotiations which would make sufficient addition to the fixed part of the wage to raise earnings to their traditional position in the Coventry league table. Needless to say, this factory had a low Topsy factor. The third example comes in between and concerns a factory where there was considerable bargaining activity but where (for reasons which will emerge later) the piecework system was under fairly close management control. Over the twenty years up to 1970 the average earnings of this factory had moved very slowly down the local league table so that its Topsy factor was not as high as in the first example. In 1970 the shop stewards carried out their first formal piecework negotiation with management and the result raised earnings to the city average. Both sides had recognized that non-negotiated drift was not yielding enough to keep factory average earnings in a 'reasonable' position by comparison with others.

Over a period of years most earnings, whether considered by region, industry, factory or whatever, move fairly parallel to each other. Percentage differentials remain fairly constant over time. Firms maintain their position by increases in N, F and G. The argument is that the component G is the prime mover in this process (at least for piecework systems) and that F consists primarily in compensatory awards to restore disrupted differentials. This important question of causation will be taken up again later. For the moment, enough has been said to demonstrate that non-negotiated drift is of great interest to a study of piecework wage determination.

The Influence of the Level of Economic Activity

LONG-TERM CHANGES

It is all too easy in discussing the economy since the Second World War to forget the relatively high level of employment that has prevailed. For those in work, changes in the level of unemployment have had less significance than for those in the depressed pre-War economy. Under high unemployment the bargaining power of workers tended to be weak and that of management correspondingly strong. A graphic account of piecework value determination under these conditions is given by Williams in his account of a railway workshop at the turn of the century.[5] He describes

[5] A. Williams, *Life in a Railway Factory,* first published 1915, Newton Abbott: David and Charles, 1969, p. 183.

how 'The pace was forced and quickened by degrees to the uttermost and then the new prices were fixed, the managers themselves attending and timing operatives and supervising the prices.' Star workers would be selected for work study and would be urged to their maximum exertions. 'If the acute manager happened to make a slight misjudgement and give (the worker) a fair price, one or other of the shed over-seers—though always very flip with him to his face—rushed off privately and informed about it and had it cut down to the dead level. Very often the overseers competed with each other to see which could make the lowest quotation in order to get into favour with the managers.'

By contrast, Lupton's description of ratefixing in an engin-eering workshop during the 1950s[6] shows vividly how full employment can turn the tables. The men he observed were adept at pulling the wool over the ratefixer's eyes and they colluded with their foreman in 'fiddling' their earnings. The self-confident workforce drove one ratefixer to com-plain: 'If we make a mistake and give you an easy time you cross-book.[7] If we make a mistake and give you a tight time you raise hell until we alter it. You want it both ways.'

It is undoubtedly the case that the major changes in the level of unemployment that have been experienced over the last century have affected bargaining behaviour profoundly. But, since the Second War, the level of employment has been comparatively high and stable. Have the relatively minor changes in the demand for labour over this recent period influenced piecework bargaining significantly?

POST-WAR FLUCTUATIONS IN UNEMPLOYMENT

There are broadly two sorts of reason for supposing that the level of economic activity might *a priori* be expected to influence the rate of piecework wage drift. The first

---

[6] T. Lupton, *On the Shop Floor*, London: Pergamon Press, 1963.

[7] 'Cross-booking' is the term applied to the misrecording of the time spent on successive jobs in order to conceal the relatively high earnings made on 'slack' job values.

emphasizes the role of the labour market. Its 'tightness' might be expected to influence the extent to which managers are willing to let wages drift upwards when they are taking on labour. It might also be expected to influence the 'aggressiveness' of pieceworkers in bargaining in-so-far as it influences their senses of job security. The second sort of explanation concentrates upon more parochial pressures within the firm. According to this an upswing in the level of production within the factory will lead to increased piece-work bargaining opportunities and increased pressure upon management controls. A downswing, on the other hand, might lead workers to spin work out. The distinction between these explanations is one of emphasis. They are not incompatible. But, while the first relies upon the price mechanism of the labour market, the second is more concerned with pressures arising from the product market.

Only a small part of the large economic literature on the relation between the rate of change of earnings and the level of employment has concerned itself specifically with wage drift. The studies that have are in broad agreement. Those of Gillion[8] and Knowles and Robinson[9] both found the rate of change of wage gap weakly associated with the rate of change of unemployment. Although Sloane[10] found no significant relationship, Marquand[11] found that 'drift was significantly related to the rate of change of unemployment over a period including the three months *subsequent* to the period in which drift arose.' In sympathy with the second explanation suggested above she concluded that 'changes at workshop level (of the demand for labour) tend to occur some time before there is any impact on the level of un-

[8] C. Gillion, 'Wage-rates, Earnings and Wage Drift', *National Institute of Economic and Social Research Review*, November 1968.

[9] K. G. J. C. Knowles and D. Robinson, 'Wage Movements in Coventry', *Bulletin of the Oxford Institute of Economics and Statistics*, 1969.

[10] Sloane, *op. cit.*, ' . . . little correlation was found between changes in employment and wage drift'.

[11] J. Marquand, 'Wage Drift: Origins, Measurement and Behaviour', *Woolwich Economic Papers* No 14, 1968.

employment (or vacancies). It is the situation in the establishment rather than in the labour market outside that is likely to provide the predominant influence upon bargains struck at establishment level.'

The test conducted for this study used the hourly earnings (less overtime) of some 10,000 skilled workers in approximately 24 engineering firms in the Coventry district from 1953 to 1970. Of these about 97 per cent were pieceworkers and most of these were on individual piecework with no systematic work study basis. An earlier study[12] gave the background of the now terminated Coventry Toolroom Agreement from which these data come.[13] In it were discussed the problems associated with the definition of skill and the treatment of overtime. It also noted the unique position of Coventry in containing the highest paying concentration of engineering firms in the country.

Over the period 1953 to 1972 only one fifth of all increases in these average piecework earnings came from national negotiations and, to judge from a regression analysis, increases in nationally prevailing rates had no impact upon the rate of change of wage gap. Consequently, the earnings movements to be explained arise primarily from plant bargaining. In some factories there had been no negotiated wage drift over the whole period, the entire wage gap had come from non-negotiated drift. These 'high Topsy' factories tended to be the higher paying ones. Other factories with less non-negotiated drift had negotiated additions to the pieceworkers' wages at plant level. As a result the wage gap measured here in consideration of the average district earnings figure was $(F + G)$ in the earlier terminology.

A variety of regression analyses were tried to test the relationship between the rate of change of earnings and of

[12] W. A. Brown, 'Piecework Wage Determination in Coventry', *Scottish Journal of Political Economy*, February 1971.

[13] The Coventry and District Engineering Employers' Association kindly supplied the wage data for this study. The unemployment data came from the Coventry office of the Department of Employment.

wage gap[14] on the one hand and both the level and the rate of change of unemployment in the Coventry district on the other. These were tried for monthly, quarterly and six-monthly data and with a variety of lags and leads. The results were broadly in line with the earlier analyses. The level of unemployment was not a significant explanatory factor but its rate of change was. The results implied that if, in the course of a year, the number of unemployed was to fall by 10 per cent this would be accompanied by the annual rate of change of wage gap being approximately 0.3 per cent higher than if unemployment remained constant. The implied increase in the rate of change of earnings on the same basis was approximately 0.2 per cent. Conversely, an increase in the number unemployed would be associated with similar decreases in the rate of change of wage gap or of earnings. These results associated changes in wages only with changes in unemployment going on concurrently. Further, when the 1953–70 period was split in two, the unemployment term proved to be significant only for the earlier, 1953–60 period. The impact of unemployment, in short, has been diminishing.[15]

[14] To simplify the calculation the measures used were not those defined earlier. They were, for monthly and quarterly data, $\dfrac{(F+G)_t - (F+G)_{(t-1)}}{(F+G)_{(t-1)}}$ and, for six monthly and for the quarterly test reported in footnote 15, $\dfrac{(N+F+G)_t - (N+F+G)_{(t-1)}}{(N+F+G)_{(t-1)}}$. However, given the relative unimportance of N, there is no reason to suppose that these measures provide misleading results for this analysis.

[15] If the rate of change of earnings is represented by $(\dot{W})$ and the rate of change of unemployment by $(\dot{U})$ and time periods by subscripts, then the results of the regression analysis carried out with quarterly data can be expressed as:

$$\dot{W}_t = 1{\cdot}037 - 0{\cdot}001\dot{U}_{(t-1)} - 0{\cdot}018\dot{U}_t - 0{\cdot}001\dot{U}_{(t+1)}$$
$$(122{\cdot}4) \qquad (0{\cdot}10) \qquad (3{\cdot}14) \qquad (0{\cdot}18)$$

where the 't' values are in brackets. The R^2 term is $0{\cdot}15$ and the Durbin-Watson statistic of autocorrelation is $2{\cdot}02$. Thus 15 per cent of variation is accounted for. Tests with six-monthly and monthly data obtained very similar coefficients for the $\dot{U}_t$ term although the amount of variation explained (respectively 18 per cent and 4 per cent) differed.

When unemployment in the Coventry district has swung up or down, it seems safe to conclude, the rate of increase of wages (and of wage gap) of skilled pieceworkers has slowed or quickened in weak response. But did this happen in all factories? Data to test this were available on the average hourly earnings (excluding overtime) of skilled production (sometimes called direct) workers from a number of firms in the area. Nineteen of these were selected whose records covered all or most of the period 1953 to 1970. Between them they covered some 95 per cent (that is, nearly 10,000) of workers whose earnings contribute to the Toolroom Rate average. It is safe to assume that the number of these who are not on piecework is negligible.

The rate of change of factory average earnings (excluding overtime) was tested against the rate of change of unemployment in the district in the same period with both six-monthly and three-monthly data. With the quarterly data it was also tested with a one period lag and a one period lead on the unemployment term. The results of the regression analysis with the current time period quarterly data are given in the left-hand half of Table 2:2. They show, first, the coefficient of the unemployment term which indicates the strength with which a change in the rate of change of unemployment is likely to be reflected in the rate of change of earnings. Secondly, the 't' value indicates whether that coefficient is statistically significant. It will be significant for the amount of data used in this case if t is greater than 1.65 at the 90 per cent level of significance, and at the 95 per cent level if it is greater than 2.00. Thirdly, the co-

---

When the period was split the following results were obtained:

1953–60 $\dot{W}_t = 1\cdot036 + 0\cdot000\dot{U}_{(t-1)} - 0\cdot022\dot{U}_t + 0\cdot002\dot{U}_{(t+1)}$
$\qquad\qquad (79\cdot58)\ (0\cdot04) \qquad\quad (2\cdot56) \qquad (0\cdot21)$
$\qquad\qquad\qquad\qquad\qquad\qquad\qquad\qquad R^2 = 0\cdot19 \qquad \text{D.W.} = 2\cdot29$

1961–70 $\dot{W}_t = 1\cdot040 - 0\cdot005\dot{U}_{(t-1)} - 0\cdot009\dot{U}_t - 0\cdot009\dot{U}_{(t+1)}$
$\qquad\qquad (91\cdot12)\ (0\cdot61) \qquad\quad (1\cdot03) \qquad (1\cdot03)$
$\qquad\qquad\qquad\qquad\qquad\qquad\qquad\qquad R^2 = 0\cdot13 \qquad \text{D.W.} = 1\cdot30$

It is evident that the well-defined relationship of the 1950s has become weak and blurred (and has significant autocorrelation) in the 1960s.

efficient of determination R^2 indicates the proportion of the total variation in the one variable explained by the other. For example, an R^2 of 0.25 would indicate that 25 per cent of the variation is so explained.

TABLE 2:2

Relationship between Rate of Change of Earnings of Skilled Pieceworkers (excluding overtime) and the Rates of Change of Unemployment and Direct Manpower
Nineteen Coventry Factories, quarterly data, 1953 to 1970

Plant	Rate of change of UNEMPLOYMENT			Rate of change of DIRECT MANPOWER		
	coefficient	't' value	R^2	coefficient	't' value	R^2
1	−0·016	1·97	0·05	0·140	2·62	0·08
2	−0·009	1·11	0·02	0·004	0·24	0·00
3	−0·009	1·29	0·03	0·005	0·19	0·00
4	−0·026	3·49	0·15	0·007	0·13	0·00
5	−0·009	0·94	0·01	−0·015	0·33	0·00
6	−0·011	2·02	0·06	−0·014	0·43	0·00
7	−0·017	1·22	0·02	0·021	0·21	0·00
8	−0·027	2·83	0·12	0·119	5·19	0·31
9	−0·000	0·05	0·00	0·051	1·68	0·05
10	−0·037	4·15	0·20	0·150	2·36	0·07
11	−0·026	2·34	0·07	−0·009	0·11	0·00
12	−0·004	0·58	0·00	0·002	0·08	0·00
13	−0·036	3·69	0·17	0·073	2·86	0·10
14	−0·014	1·33	0·02	−0·005	0·09	0·00
15	−0·012	1·17	0·02	0·200	3·84	0·16
16	−0·017	1·87	0·05	0·036	0·70	0·01
17	−0·009	0·91	0·01	−0·035	0·88	0·01
18	−0·015	1·65	0·05	0·111	2·06	0·07
19	−0·023	2·26	0·09	0·168	3·21	0·16

It will be seen that, of the nineteen firms, seven have a relationship between the wage and unemployment variables that is significant at the 95 per cent level and another three have a significant one at the 90 per cent level. All the other firms had a negative coefficient for the unemployment term. The amount of variation explained was up to 20 per cent. The relationships imply that a 10 per cent increase (or decrease) in the number of unemployed in the district will, for the ten firms with significant results, be associated with the annual rate of average hourly skilled piecework earnings being lower (or higher) by between 0.11 and 0.37 per cent than would otherwise be the case with no change in unemployment.

As might be expected from the experience with the aggregate data, tests for an effect upon wages of the unemployment term with a lead and a lag of three months produce less positive results. But they do produce some. Interestingly, these are fairly evenly balanced. A change in unemployment *precedes* by one quarter an associated change in the rate of earnings increase at three plants at 95 per cent significance levels and a further two at 90 per cent significance levels. It *follows* at one quarter earnings changes at three firms at 95 per cent significance levels and a further three at 90 per cent. The impact of unemployment changes upon wages at the level of the plant is, in fact, fairly diffuse.

A fair conclusion would seem to be that the sensitivity of piecework earnings to changes in the local level of unemployment varies from plant to plant in both strength and timing. While such sensitivity is fairly widespread it is also fairly weak. It also appears to have been diminishing over the last two decades. Individual piecework bargaining was largely unaffected by labour market fluctuations in the 1960s.

THE LEVEL OF ACTIVITY WITHIN THE FACTORY

In order to consider the impact of domestic variations in the level of activity upon the rate of increase of a plant's earnings, it is necessary to have some indicator of this level. Because products and product mixes change, the level of production does not help here. But one figure that was available for all nineteen firms is the number of skilled production (or direct) workers employed. Although in the short-run firms may on the one hand use overtime working and on the other hand hoard labour to accommodate fluctuations in production, over the period of eighteen years under consideration and with quarterly data the level of direct manpower is likely to be a fairly accurate indicator of the level of activity. Any increases in labour-saving capital equipment are likely to have been fairly gradual.

The second half of Table 2:2 provides the results of a regression analysis of the rate of change of piecework earnings against the rate of change of direct manpower. For none of the nineteen plants had the *level* of direct manpower provided a significant relationship with the rate of change of earnings. But it is clear from the table that the *rate of change* of direct manpower is more interesting. Seven of the plants have significant results at the 95 per cent level and another at the 90 per cent level. It is evident that for many factories the explanatory power of manpower changes is less than that of unemployment changes. The signs carried by the coefficients are also less consistent.

On a closer look it can be seen that for six of the eight plants where the manpower relationship is significant, the explanatory power of that relationship is greater than that of the corresponding relationship with the unemployment variable. From this it seems fair to conclude that although it is less common for a plant's earnings to be sensitive to its own changes in manpower than to changes in local unemployment, where they *are* sensitive to manpower changes this relationship explains more variation than unemployment changes. In these plants, it appears, the fortunes of the plant itself have a greater impact upon wages than do the fortunes of the labour market outside.

On the most simple assumptions there is an obvious relationship between the expansion of a firm's labour force and the diminution in the number of unemployed outside. Because of this one would expect those firms' earnings which are sensitive to changes in unemployment also to be sensitive to changes in manpower. But the traces of this relationship are very weak and are not significant at the 90 per cent level. The presence of these traces suggests that there might be multicollinearity between the unemployment and manpower terms; that is, they might be correlated to one another in such a way that the results of Table 2:2 would be misleading. In fact, however, when they were tested in the same equation the coefficients and 't' values changed very little. When the manpower term was regressed against the unemployment term with a one quarter lead and lag and in the current period, only a minority of firms showed a significant relationship and it explained little of the variance. There was no relationship at all between those firms whose rate of change of manpower was correlated with changes in earnings, on the one hand, and those for which it was related to changes in unemployment on the other.

It was observed earlier that a sensitivity of earnings movements to the level of economic activity could be a reflection of pressures acting in the labour market or it could be a reflection of more parochial forces at the level of the factory. A simple hypothesis following from the second of these would be that, if the parochial forces are the ones that matter, any relationship between changes in unemployment and earnings that is observed is merely a reflection of this, representing the aggregate of what is happening at many plants but not revealing any causal relationship. This simple hypothesis can now be rejected; the influence of the unemployment term upon earnings is sufficiently independent of that of the manpower term for two distinct effects to be identified. Earnings, it appears, can be influenced both by variations in the local labour market and by variations in the level of activity within the plant.

The mechanisms bringing these effects about will receive attention in the next section. For the moment it is of interest to examine the special cases of plants 1 and 15 in the Table. With the quarterly analysis presented here it can be seen that these two plants show some of the most sensitive of relations between earnings and manpower movements. This is far more marked when the regressions are carried out with six-monthly data. Then the manpower expression for the two firms account for, respectively, 30 per cent and 42 per cent of variation in earnings and for no other plant does it account for more than 17 per cent. These two firms are interesting for another reason. Over the period considered the rank order of the nineteen firms in terms of their average earnings has been fairly constant. There have been very few rapid or major shifts up and down the 'league table'. But firms 1 and 15 are distinguished not only for having executed the most impressive leaps in rank order but also for having jumped to the top of the league table. Firm 1 had spent many years around the twelfth position until 1953 when it rose, in the space of half a year, to become the highest paying of all. It remained in that position with barely an interruption until 1966 when it was displaced into second place by firm 15. Firm 15 had occupied a traditional position even further down the league table; for the previous decade it had remained between the fifteenth and eighteenth position in order of earnings levels until in the course of late 1965 it rocketed to the top position and remained there until the data ceased to be collected in 1971.

After the results reported it will not be surprising that these extraordinary jumps in the earnings levels of firms 1 and 15 were accompanied by large and rapid expansions in the direct manpower employed. In the case of one firm this was a response to the increase in demand for the product arising from the government's rearmament programme. In the other firm's case it accompanied a major breakthrough into a lucrative export market. This may be thought to provide sufficient explanation; the rapid rise in wages may be seen as the deliberate managerial response to a rapid increase in their demand for labour. But this does not provide the answer. For at least eight of the nineteen firms experienced, at one time or another, expansions in their labour forces at least as rapid and at least as great as those apparently aberrant ones of firms 1 and 15.[16]

---

[16] Firms 1 and 15 expanded their direct skilled labour forces by, respectively, 22 per cent and 20 per cent in the two six-month periods discussed. Other firms experienced increases in direct skilled labour over the same period of 50, 70 and even 90 per cent. In fact, although these increases were exceptional for firms 1 and 15, they were not at all unusual in comparison with other firms. The accompanying earnings increases were exceptional however, being the two greatest experienced by any firms over six months over the period. Firms 1 and 15 were medium to small employers and did

These other firms were in the same labour market for approximately the same skilled engineering labour. If market forces were to explain the extraordinary rises in the earnings of firms 1 and 15, why do these other firms not have the same experience? If other firms could expand their labour forces without raising their earnings dramatically it is unlikely that it was deliberate management policy that forced up wages in 1 and 15. The explanation is more likely to lie in a collapse of cost controls or of ratefixing arising from the rise in the level of production and a deeper explanation is likely to come from the nature of the product markets which permit managements to survive with such fragile control systems.

The examples of these two plants demonstrate in an extreme way how changes in a product market can feed through to influence wage movements. A brief consideration of the range of product markets involved in any random selection of engineering factories will show the very different pressures that can come to bear on wages. Among the nineteen factories considered here some were on a crude 'cost-plus' pricing basis whereby an increase in the wage bill automatically led to increased profits. Others were jobbing contractors who had to price on a fiercely competitive basis. For some, wage-costs were under a quarter of value added; for others they were over three-quarters and their managements were of necessity more preoccupied with wage control. Some factories sold long-lasting capital goods largely on their technical reputation and after-sales service, with price a secondary factor; others sold consumer goods in fickle and highly price-elastic markets. The impact of this diversity upon management controls and bargaining behaviour will be taken up in the last chapter. For the moment it is sufficient

---

not require special skills. In any case, there are reasons for supposing that the Coventry labour market is exceptionally flexible in its definition of skill (see Brown, *op. cit.*). The timing of the expansions of these two firms cannot be taken as an explanation of their earnings experience. Other firms carried out equivalent or greater expansions at the same time.

to note that it helps an understanding of the uneven influence of changes in manpower upon the piecework earnings of different factories.

There is, as was discussed earlier, nothing incompatible about theories that explain wage movements in terms of labour market forces and those that do so in terms of the product market. Both appear to have some explanatory value. When product markets are so diverse any interaction between them and the labour market is likely to have a complex effect on wages. If this study tends to stress the importance of the product market it does so partly to redress an imbalance of attention.

THE OVERT CAUSES OF EARNINGS FLUCTUATIONS

If these cyclical variations in the level of economic activity influence the rate of change of earnings in some factories, in what changes in behaviour are they manifest? The market for labour differs from, say, the market for vegetables not least because a vegetable has no power to influence its price nor (so far as one is aware) any aspiration to do so. In factories with fairly stable workforces an alteration in the rate of change of earnings is likely to result from some explicit alteration in bargaining behaviour which, in turn, may arise from a change in the level of activity in the factory or the economy.

Although the evidence shows that variation in the level of employment in the local labour market has a weak effect upon piecework wage drift, it is difficult to perceive the changes in behaviour that bring this about. In the context of piecework it is particularly difficult to see how managers could react deliberately to adjust wages to market forces. As subsequent analysis will demonstrate, managers in factories with aggressive labour forces appear to exercise little effective control over piecework bargaining and are most unlikely to be able to carry out short-term adjustments in earnings. On the workers' side the mechanism is a little clearer. There have been times—in Coventry the sharp recession in the car industry in 1966 is the clearest example—

when well publicized redundancies made workers more cautious in factories not directly affected. It appears that anxiety about their job security at times of worsening unemployment may make pieceworkers work slower or push less hard.[17] But this reaction is by no means clear-cut.

It is easier to find anecdotal evidence demonstrating how fluctuations in the level of activity within a factory can influence its earnings movements. The extreme cases of factories 1 and 15 can be augmented by one of the case studies where it was clear that wages in one department rose dramatically because of the introduction of a new product. The rush with which the new product was pushed into production led to 'slack' piecework values being fixed by an over-worked ratefixing department. Lerner has observed[18] how the introduction of new products and models provides fresh opportunities for piecework bargaining. To this can be added the observation that workers tend to guard against inflation by pushing for a more generous value for a job which they expect will last a long time. The expected life of new models may be important.

Even a detailed knowledge of the domestic circumstances of a plant may, however, not be enough to permit prediction of earnings movements. For instance, a decline in the level of activity of a factory is often accompanied by short-time working in some departments. Those on short-time may then increase their level of effort and their hourly earnings in an attempt to maintain the standard of living to which they are accustomed. Those who fear short-time may slow down to avoid it by spinning work out. Those who know themselves to be safe may work on as normal. In short, reactions to a change in production can be very varied.

It might be thought that the level of overtime being

[17] Against this it should be noted that in late 1971 Coventry experienced its most massive strike since the War at the time of highest unemployment since the War although, in contesting the employers' revoking of the Toolroom Agreement, the AUEW was acting defensively.

[18] S. W. Lerner, 'Wage Drift, Wage Fixing and Drift Statistics', *Manchester School*, 1965.

worked would influence the efforts of pieceworkers and consequently their hourly earnings. Among pieceworkers overtime tends to be limited in scale and fluctuations.[19] Two tests were carried out for a relationship between the level of and changes in overtime on the one hand and the rate of change of wage gap on the other. The first test was conducted for average overtime for all direct workers for two factories and yielded no significant result. The second test took disaggregated departmental data for a third factory. A variety of tests on weekly data over the course of a year found weak but significant results for three out of six departments and, of these, one was perverse—that is, it implied that an increase in overtime working was accompanied by an increase in effort. It seems fair to conclude that if any relationship exists between overtime and piecework earnings, it is weak and elusive.

There is one cause of fluctuation in earnings that deserves comment because it is widespread and because it indicates the extent to which pieceworkers can regulate their earnings in the short-run. This is the phenomenon of 'bull-week'. Before the summer holiday and (to a lesser extent) before Christmas pieceworkers tend to increase their efforts and/or boost their earnings from 'the back of the book'. At one factory where an increase in effort was the only way of doing this, individual effort rose by an average of four per cent from its long term level in bull-week. Where 'saved' piecework earnings could be cashed from 'the back of the book', the bull-week boost to earnings was regularly 15 per cent above average in some factories.

The Influence of Changes in Productivity

Variations in the level of activity within firms and within

[19] Mackay *et al.* found that for their sample of Birmingham factories the average overtime worked by pieceworkers 'only once exceeded three hours'. (D. Robinson (ed) *Local Labour Markets and Wage Structures*, Gower Press, London: 1970, p. 147). For the factories in the current study the average would also appear generally to be between two to three hours.

the economy are likely to influence earnings movements only in a short-term cyclical way.[20] The most obvious explanation of the long-term upward trend of non-negotiated piecework drift might be thought to lie in increasing productivity. This could be an important factor leading to differences in the rate of wage drift between different firms. As was discussed earlier, under perfect work study, piecework earnings should only increase as a result of increased operator effort or negotiated increases in wage rates. But in practice increases in output per man arising from technical innovation can slip by the work study engineer and can increase the pieceworker's earnings without him increasing his level of effort or of skill.

A famous controversy between Turner and Lerner[21] was largely concerned with the joint questions of the extent to which pieceworkers' wage drift was accompanied by increases in productivity and whether or not these were the result of increased skill and effort or were 'windfall' gains to the workers. Because these authors used industry level measures of productivity they were unable to separate out different sources of productivity increase. But these sources may be very important. An automating innovation for instance, may increase labour productivity considerably

[20] If it is the case, as has been suggested above, that the product market must play an important part in an explanation of plant-level wage determination, one would expect variations in plant profits to contribute to an explanation of cyclical changes in the rate of increase in wage gap. The earlier study (Brown, *op. cit.*) tested in a fairly simple way for any relationship between the rate of change of non-negotiated wage gap and both the level and the rate of change of profits (for various time periods) for two factories. Although it perceived no relationship and despite the many statistical problems raised by profits data this deserves further investigation.

[21] S. W. Lerner and J. Marquand, 'Workshop Bargaining, Wage Drift and Productivity in the British Engineering Industry', *Manchester School* 1962; Lerner *op. cit.* 1965; H. A. Turner, 'Wages: Industry Rates, Workplace Rates and the Wage Drift', *Manchester School*, 1956; H. A. Turner, 'Wages, Productivity and the Level of unemployment: more on the "Wage Drift" ', *Manchester School*, 1960; H. A. Turner, 'The Disappearing Drift (or, in Defence of Turner)', *Manchester School*, 1964: H. A. Turner, 'That Damned Drift: a note on the Turner-Lerner controversy', *Manchester School*, 1967.

without influencing piecework earnings while an improvement in the quality of raw materials might increase earnings considerably as a windfall gain.

The relationship between productivity increases and piecework wage drift can have a little more light cast on it by considering completely disaggregated data on changes in direct unit labour costs. Data on the cost of the pieceworkers' labour input to an unchanging product, taken with data on the pieceworkers' wage earnings over time, enable one to calculate the change in hours of direct labour input per unit of physical output (which can be taken as a definition of labour productivity). A further refinement that can be introduced where work study information is reliable is to consider the standard labour input per unit of output. This enables one to calculate the proportion of the change in direct labour hours input that results from labour saving (usually) technical improvements as opposed to that which results from 'improved' labour inputs such as increased effort, skill or ingenuity.

Unfortunately, it is difficult to find firms with accounting data permitting even the first stage of this calculation, and it is harder still to find ones which have produced an identical product over a number of years. For this study adequate data were available for firms A, B, H and K. As can be seen from Table 2:1, the first two had a relatively high and the last two a relatively low rate of non-negotiated wage drift. The products chosen from each required many score different manufacturing operations and passed through most of the major sections of their respective factories. Consequently the direct labour costs that they incurred on the way came from a typical cross-section of production workers.

Details of the calculations involved for firms A and B are given elsewhere.[22] For A it was calculated that, over a six year period, an annual compound rate of increase of average hourly piecework earnings of direct skilled workers

[22] Brown, *op. cit.*

of 6.5 per cent was accompanied by an annual compound rate of increase of physical output per manhour of direct skilled labour of approximately 3.2 per cent. The management estimated that most, and possibly all, of this increase in productivity was accounted for by technical innovation and changes in organization. For firm B the equivalent annual rates of increase over a period of nine years were for earnings 5.8 per cent accompanied by 2.6 per cent for physical output per direct manhour. Again, for B considerable technical innovation was likely to have accounted for the bulk of increases in productivity.

Work study data were available for factory H. Here over a four year period there was a non-negotiated piecework wage drift of 1.8 per cent and an increase in physical output per manhour of 2.0 per cent—both annual compound rates. When it was taken into account that one quarter of the increase in physical output per manhour came from explicit changes in technique by management, the increase in productivity resulting from 'improved' labour input accounted for only one half of the non-negotiated wage drift. Analysis of the data from factory K over a two year period was complicated by the fact that productivity declined by some 3 per cent per year despite a countervailing improvement from technical innovation of $\frac{1}{2}$ per cent. Overall, an annual non-negotiated piecework wage drift of 1 per cent was accompanied by a decline in labour input with the effect that the rate of non-negotiated wage drift not covered by increasing physical output per manhour was between one and two per cent per year. The fact that labour inputs 'improved' for H and 'deteriorated' for K can be explained largely by the fact that labour turnover at K was twice the magnitude of that at H. The more stable workforce at H was probably able to benefit more from 'learning curve' improvements.

The first point to be made on the basis of these figures is that only a part of non-negotiated piecework wage drift appears to be associated with increases in productivity. Secondly, only a part of these increases in productivity—

and in some cases a very small part—is associated with 'improved' labour inputs in terms of greater effort, skill or ingenuity on the part of pieceworkers. Thirdly, it appears to be the case that not only is a high level of windfall gains associated with a high level of non-negotiated wage drift (which is to some extent necessarily true) but also that a high level of windfall gains is associated with a high level of drift which arises for reasons wholly unrelated to productivity increases. Put another way, in a factory where workers are able to reap above average rewards from technical innovation without 'improving' their labour input, they are also likely to be getting above average earnings increases from other sources (notably by bargaining pressure). The reasons for this will receive attention in Chapter Four.

The conclusion is similar to that of the section dealing with the impact of the level of activity upon piecework wage drift. Once again the economic variable explains a relatively small part of what is required for an understanding of piecework wage determination. This appears to be true both for the rate of drift over time and also for the different drift rates of different factories.

3

The Dynamics of Internal Wage Structures

A study of a system of bargaining would be very incomplete without an analysis of the pay structures that it brings about. A pay structure can be defined as a description of the relative pay levels of individuals or groups and such structures are influenced by forces beyond domestic bargaining institutions. Theorists have noted that '. . . the determinateness of a particular internal wage structure depends upon the strength of competitive forces in the labor market, the restraint exerted by the product market, and upon the nature of the union and bargaining system.'[1] In attempting to explain how the outside market influences the internal wage structure they have introduced notions of 'wage clusters' and 'key jobs'.[2] In accounting for some of the internal wage structure's apparent autonomy they have stressed the importance of 'job specificity' of on-the-job training and of custom.[3]

Empirical studies of the operation of local labour markets in the British engineering industry confirm that the processes at work in wage determination must be complex. Robinson and MacKay and their colleagues have found disorderly interplant wage structures that appeared to be singularly

[1] G. H. Hildebrand, 'External Influences and the Determination of the Internal Wage Structure', in J. L. Meij (ed), *Internal Wage-Structure*, Amsterdam: North-Holland, 1963, p. 296.

[2] J. T. Dunlop, 'The Task of Contemporary Wage Theory', in G. W. Taylor and F. C. Pierson (eds), *New Concepts in Wage Determination*, New York: McGraw-Hill, 1967.

[3] P. B. Doeringer and M. J. Piore, *Internal Labor Markets and Manpower Analysis*, Lexington: D. C. Heath, 1971.

unresponsive to short run changes in labour market conditions.[4] On looking inside plants it was concluded that '... the outstanding characteristic of the earnings relativities which prevail in any plant is that they are unique; there appear to be as many internal wage structures as there are plants.'[5] Further, '... changes over time in intra-plant differentials do not appear to be responsive to market forces as measured by the demand/supply conditions for different types of labour'.[6] But an analysis of variance did reveal that 'the most important factor determining an individual's increase in earnings was the plant rather than the occupational group in which he was employed.'[7]

It appears, then, that labour market pressures exercise relatively little constraint upon the internal wage structure of engineering firms. There appears to be ample scope for a more detailed study of the wage determination process to discern the parochial forces at work and also the mechanisms whereby product market pressures make themselves felt. This chapter will first describe the wage structures that develop under piecework and then attempt to explain them.

More on the Nature of the Bargaining Process

Before embarking upon a statistical analysis of piecework wage structures it will be helpful to analyse the bargaining process further in order to develop some testable hypotheses about them. The type of piecework system on which this analysis will concentrate is the type occurring in factories with high Topsy factors. In these hot-house conditions the characteristics of non-negotiated bargaining sprout and flourish most interestingly. The anomalies and distortions

[4] See D. Robinson, *Wage Drift, Fringe Benefits and Manpower Distribution*, OECD, 1968; D. Robinson (ed), *Local Labour Markets and Wage Structures, op. cit.*: D. I. MacKay, D. Boddy, J. Brack, J. A. Diack, N. Jones, *Labour Markets under Different Employment Conditions*, London: George Allen and Unwin, 1971.

[5] MacKay, *et al., op cit.*, p. 118.

[6] *ibid.*, p. 130.

[7] *ibid.*, p. 130.

that become established in piecework systems under close managerial control are usually modest versions of those that bloom where the Topsy factor is high.

THE FREQUENCY OF BARGAINING

The frequency with which workers can bargain or rebargain their job values has an obvious effect upon the control that they have over their earnings. This was mentioned, particularly in relation to production technology, by Lerner and Marquand.[8] The next chapter will establish a connection between the prevailing custom and practice rules within a plant and the frequency of bargaining. At first sight it seems a simple and obvious step to test the relationship between bargaining frequency and Topsy. In practice, difficulties occur.

Technical factors influence the frequency of bargains but this need not necessarily affect the rate of non-negotiated drift. For example, there can be little doubt that more fresh job values are fixed per worker per week in the low Topsy firms H, J and K than in the firms A, F and G which have much higher drift. An important distinction must be made between bargains that occur because it is technically necessary to fix a new job value and those that occur on a more dubious pretext because the pieceworker is pushing for more money. Unfortunately (but understandably) factory records do not usually recognize this distinction which is, in any case, not clear-cut.

It is also impossible to assess the impact of a single piecework bargain upon the future earnings of the workers involved. Such a bargain may affect a small part of a short one-off job affecting one worker. At the other extreme it might be the sole determinant of the earnings of a large number of workers for a long time. These facts prevent much meaning being attached to an aggregate number of piecework bargains or its use as a determinant of drift.

Despite these difficulties, it would be useful to have some

[8] S. Lerner and J. Marquand, *op. cit.*, 1962, p. 52.

indication of the frequency with which an average piece-worker might be expected to be involved in a bargain. Those factories with adequate records or candid ratefixers provided a basis for this. At A, where there were few operators working on similar machines so that a single price change usually affected only one man, there were on average some 70 new values fixed per week with at least three-quarters of them being simple revaluations of unchanged jobs. With a pieceworking labour force of approximately 200 the average individual could thus expect a changed job value approximately every three weeks. At F with 2200 pieceworkers there were some 100 fresh values fixed each week. Many of these affected more than one person immediately and a reasonable estimate would be that the average individual received a fresh job value every seven weeks. One half of these were explicitly reobservations of unchanged jobs. Similar estimates produced the figure of once in four weeks for B, of once in eight weeks for E and once in seven weeks for G. For each of the last three it is a conservative estimate that at least half of negotiations were reobservations of unchanged jobs.

There is no need to dwell further on the problems of interpreting these figures. It seems safe to conclude that a pieceworker in a high Topsy factory can expect, on average, to have a fresh job value every one or two months and the majority of these are likely to arise for reasons other than technical necessity. In short, these pieceworkers have regular opportunities to adjust their earnings.

KEY ASPECTS OF THE BARGAIN

The next chapter will be concerned with the nature and variety of the different custom and practice rules that govern the conduct of the piecework bargain. It will be established there that, in factories with high Topsy factors, the individual pieceworker is in a position of considerable power. If he fails to agree a job value with the ratefixer he will be paid at or close to his past average earnings. Thus such a failure to agree will cost the worker little while the

c

low effort he puts into the job in question (if he works at it at all) will frustrate management's production plans. Put against this there is an obligation on the worker, that will probably be brought to his notice by his shop steward if he fails to observe it himself, not to 'push things too far'. An undue strain on the day-to-day working relationships that the pieceworker has with junior management could lose him many personal favours that he values. In the long run it could bring more drastic intervention from senior management.

Bargaining is carried out over two distinct aspects of the job. The first is the time within which the man might be expected to carry out the job when working at a 'reasonable' effort—that is, the 'floor-to-floor time'. The ratefixer requires skill and experience to estimate this in the face of likely attempts by the worker to mislead him. The second aspect of the job which is bargained over is the level of earnings which the worker 'ought' to receive on the new job value. Both sides are likely to argue over this in terms of fair comparisons.

Thus the level of earnings which the pieceworker finally gets depends upon several factors. It will depend upon the the level of effort which he is willing to maintain and, with supervisors exerting little or no pressure on effort levels, they vary considerably between men. It will depend upon the pieceworker's success in fooling the ratefixer on floor-to-floor times and the extent to which the technical features of the job help in this. Another factor is the aggressiveness of the worker and the extent to which he is willing to strain his relationship with junior management and his fellow workers by exploiting the system. The degree of fatalism that pieceworkers exhibit in accepting tight times without appeal and reobservation varies. So also does the latitude left by the pieceworker's success in fooling the ratefixer on floor-to-ing slack job values. Finally, it depends upon the comparisons that he uses and upon the ratefixer's sense of what would be 'fair'.

This description leaves many questions unanswered. In

the first place, the bargaining process would appear to be so unrestrained that the wage movements which result might be expected to be wholly chaotic. Secondly, this disorder might be expected to grow cumulatively. Thirdly, it is not clear to what extent individual pieceworkers take the opportunity of bargaining to 'leapfrog' their earnings over those of their peers in a competitive way. Finally, does the process permit any permanency of differentials between pieceworkers of different occupations? This list of questions reveals the extent of ignorance about the behaviour of pay under piecework. The answers will come from the statistics.

The Wage Structure

Most discussions of wage structures consider the earnings of workers as the *average* earnings of occupational groups. For most purposes there is obvious sense in this. But this discussion of the dynamics of individual piecework bargaining requires a description of how the earnings of individual workers stand and move with respect to one another. For this the main measures utilized will be those of the scatter of earnings and the ranking of earnings. Overtime will be excluded partly because pieceworkers tend not to work much of it and partly because the overtime that they do work appears to be fairly consistent.[9] So far as the question of skill differentials between pieceworkers is concerned, the analysis was made relatively simple by the fact that most factories had virtually all their piece-

Both better reasons for inclusion?

[9] See D. Robertson, *Factory Wage Structures and National Agreements*, Cambridge: Cambridge University Press, 1960, p. 62; NBPI, Report No 161, *Hours of Work, Overtime and Shiftworking*, London: HMSO, 1970, p. 26.

MacKay *et al.* note (*op. cit.*, p. 147) that for their Birmingham sample of factories ' . . . in every period timeworkers averaged at least twice as many overtime hours as pieceworkers. In the former case, overtime usually averaged about six hours per week, while for pieceworkers the average only once exceeded three hours.' The factories covered in the current study were very similar in this respect.

workers in the same grade. For instance, they were almost all skilled men at A and B, semi-skilled men at F and G and semi-skilled women at J and K. Where it was more complicated at the other factories the largest homogeneous skill-grade was taken.

TABLE 3:1

The scatter of piecework earnings
The coefficient of variation of standard individual piecework earnings for a homogeneous skill grade of worker by factory

					FACTORY					
	A	B	C	D	E	F	G	H	J	K
C.V. (%)	25	14·5	n.a.	12	13·5	10	20	3	n.a.	n.a.

THE SCATTER OF EARNINGS

As Table 3:1 demonstrates, the scatter of piecework earnings for workers of a single skill grade can be wide. At factory A the coefficient of variation[10], CV, for all individually pieceworking skilled men was approximately 25 per cent during 1969. Put in more tangible terms the scatter of average hourly earnings (for one month) ranged from the lowest pieceworker's 39p to the highest's 136p. The lowest tenth of the workers earned below 60p and the highest above 115p. But, as the Table also shows, this scatter varies enormously between factories.[11]

Within a factory the scatter remains fairly constant over time. At A, for instance, over 1969 the CV of monthly average individual hourly earnings of the 145 workers remained within the limits of 24.0 and 26.8 per cent. Over

[10] The coefficient of variation is a convenient measure of the scatter of a distribution, in this case of earnings. It is the standard deviation of the distribution expressed as a percentage of the arithmetic average.

[11] The characteristic shape of the piecework earnings distribution is the symmetrical bell-shaped Normal curve. This can be tested for statistically (for example 50 per cent of the population will fall within 0·67 standard deviations either side of the average) and was found to fit fairly consistently for factories in the case studies which had suitable data (factories A, E, and F).

the longer period of 1966 to 1970 the figures for January and June ranged between 24.0 and 27.6 per cent. Those for the thirty-odd members of the machine shop ranged no farther than from 19.0 to 19.9 per cent over the same months.

Similar evidence comes from other factories. At B the scatter of individual hourly earnings of 200 skilled men for October 1966 was 14.3 per cent. For the other month sampled, February 1970, it was 14.5 per cent. For factory F and CV for between 1660 and 1800 semi-skilled men for the months of January and July from 1960 to 1970 ranged between 9.5 per cent and 11.1 per cent.

An analogous figure is the scatter of average earnings of separate shops or sections within the factory. At K the scatter for 142 sections of semi-skilled girls in July 1964 was 10.0 per cent. For the same sections in the other month sampled, November 1967, it was 9.8 per cent. Similarly for factory D, the 42 sections that could be compared between 1965 and 1967 showed CVs for the average earnings of one week of, respectively, 16 and 15 per cent.

Only one factory showed figures that were inconsistent with this remarkable stability of earnings scatter over time. That was C where the CV of bonus earnings oscillated wildly—but, as C's wage structure is remarkable in other respects it will receive closer attention later.

TABLE 3:2

Scatter of earnings in sample sections in factory D in 1968 and 1970

Sex	Occupation	Coefficient of variation (%)	
		1968	1970
male	a	18	16
male	b	11	14
female	a	4	8
female	b	9	8
female	c	15	16
female	d	8	9

Stability was also apparent within sections in factories. Although, as Table 3:2 shows, the CV can differ hugely from section to section, it tends to remain fairly constant in each section over time. Apart from the evidence of factory D given here, it was also looked for and found at factories A and B.

Generally, then, it appears that the dispersion of individual piecework earnings within a factory remains very constant over periods of several years. This suggests that piecework wage structures have some stability; if they do become cumulatively more disorderly at least they do not tend to sprawl out in the process.

THE RANKING OF EARNINGS

This leaves unclear the way in which earnings move within the bounds of the stable distribution. There are three basic possibilities. The first is that the size of the earnings increase that results from a bargain is (within limits) fairly random so that sometimes individuals will move a long way relative to their workmates' earnings and sometimes they will barely move at all. The second possibility is that when an individual pieceworker gets an opportunity to bargain he, as it were, seizes it in both hands and extracts an earnings increase that moves him to the top of the distribution in a competitive way. In the interval before he next bargains he will then find others overtaking him and so will slither down the earnings 'league table'. The third simple pattern of movement would be for individuals to gain fairly constant small increases whenever they bargain. In this way their position in the league table would not alter much as they would only change places with those workers whose earnings were traditionally close to them. To choose between these possibilities it is best to look at how the ranking of individual earnings changes from one period to the next.

The statistics available for factory A provided an opportunity to carry out the test in exceptionally stringent conditions. This factory had a high Topsy factor, heavy piecework bargaining and a poorly coordinated shop steward organization. Average hourly piecework earnings for all skilled individuals were available for the months of April

1969 and March 1970. The number of men identifiable in both periods was 120 which was about 80 per cent of those involved. This was the period of what was nationally known as a 'wage explosion' and the average earnings rose from 84p per hour to 94p per hour between the two months—an annual rate of increase of 12 per cent—during which time the frequency of bargaining may have risen above its average of one per man every three weeks or so. Despite the rapid increase in earnings, there were no abnormalities in the behaviour of its scatter. The CV only changed from 22.0 per cent to 21.4 per cent over the period.

The earnings of individuals were placed in rank order for both months and the correlation coefficient between the two rankings was calculated. It proved to be 0.88 (statistically significant at the 99 per cent level). This is notably high. It suggests strongly that, even at a time of rapid earnings increase, individuals maintain a fairly constant position in the league table of earnings. This favours the third possible pattern of movement hypothesized above.

TABLE 3: 3

Rank correlation of individual earnings within machining groups at factory A between April 1969 and March 1970

(*n* = number of men involved)

Machine type	n	rank correlation coefficient
boring	10	0·96
capstan lathes	23	0·63
drilling	23	0·82
milling	18	0·72
grinding	22	0·70

Although all the men are technically classed as skilled, they have different occupations as machinists and the average earnings of these occupational groups prove to be statistically distinct. In other words, a wage structure based on occupation is evident among the skilled pieceworkers at factory A. Although earnings in these occupational groups overlap enormously it is of interest to find whether there is much movement in their own internal league tables. The relevant rank correlation coefficients for the more distinct occupational groups is given in Table 3:3. It will be seen that, although they are generally smaller than the 0.88 for all workers, there is still a considerable uniformity of ranking. The rank order of the average earnings of the five machining sections considered in the Table remained unchanged over the period considered. Thus it appears that at least some of the stability of ranking of all individual earnings arises from a loose occupational wage structure but that, within these occupational groups, there is still considerable stability. The reasons for the occupational wage structure will be considered later.

Equivalent data were not obtained from other factories but it was possible to find how the ranking of section average earnings moved over time. If sections are found to keep their rank order over periods of several years it would suggest that no large-scale 'leapfrogging' was taking place.

The clearest evidence of this came from factory G where the sectional average earnings were available annually from 1963 to 1967 for the 30 sections of the main part of the plant. The minor part was excluded for reasons that will be discussed later in this chapter. Comparing years with 1967, the rank correlation coefficients year by year were: with 1966, 0.89; with 1965, 0.77; with 1964, 0.71; and with 1963, 0.89. Thus, despite the factory's high Topsy factor, the league-table position of the different semi-skilled machining sections remained very stable.

At factory F the rank correlation of the 16 sections of semi-skilled machinists, comparing a month in 1970 with the same month in the previous year, was 0.88. For factory D the rank correlation for the 47 comparable sections of semi-skilled workers, comparing figures for 1965 with three years earlier, was 0.77.

This evidence suggests that pieceworkers bargain in such a way that differentials between them will not be greatly altered. There are no signs of random movements and certainly not of competitive leapfrogging. It is appropriate to call this a 'stable ranking' pattern of bargaining. Where the scatter of earnings is wide, as at factory A, there is far more room for an individual's earnings to move without upsetting the ranking. The apparent prevalence of the pattern where there is individual bargaining has important implications for the analysis of piecework bargaining to which this study will return.

THE 'VINTAGE RANKING' PATTERN

The data from factory C show wages moving so very differently from those reported so far that they deserve special attention. Taking first the scatter of earnings, the CV of the bonus points[12] of the 4700 pieceworkers changed from 3.2 per cent in 1967 to 4.1 per cent in 1970. For the twelve gangs of over 80 men the CV went from 3.1 per cent in 1967 through 4.7 per cent in 1968 to 2.0 per cent in 1970. In brief, the scatter appears to fluctuate vigorously.

The behaviour of the rank correlation is equally anomalous. When the ranking of earnings of the 53 gangs with more than 20 men was compared between 1967 and 1970, the correlation was found to be insignificant. This would appear to be compatible with the hypothesis that earnings movements are largely random and that ranking is of no importance to the bargainers. A different and clearer pattern emerges, however, if the twelve gangs with more than 80 men in them are considered alone. This is done in Table 3:4 where correlations between successive years are shown. The pattern is one of considerable turmoil with a significant (at the 90 per cent level) inversion of differentials between 1969 and 1970. Statistically this behaviour appears to fit closest to the second pattern hypothesized in which bargainers seize upon the opportunities they have to push their earnings up to the top of the hierarchy in a competitive and 'leapfrogging' way. It suggests that traditional rank

[12] The scatter of bonus points at factory C is not directly comparable with the scatter of earnings because they relate to a number of different piecework bonus rates within each gang. Proportional *changes* in this scatter, however, give an unbiassed guide to the changes in the overall scatter of earnings.

orders and differentials do not carry much weight in the bargain. Why should factory C differ so much from the others in this respect?

TABLE 3:4

Rank correlation of earnings of 12 gangs of 80 men at factory C

Period of comparison	Rank correlation coefficient
1967 on 1969	0·40
1968 on 1969	0·65
1967 on 1970	−0·45
1968 on 1970	−0·23
1969 on 1970	−0·51

Factory C is a large car assembly plant and, unlike the other nine factories, the piecework system is predominantly based on gangs. Most of the gangs are large (with more than twenty men) and a fresh job value affects the earnings of all members of the gang even if only one of them does the job in question. At this plant—as at many other car assembly plants—it is a custom and practice rule that fresh negotiations on job values will take place only when a new model is introduced. Thus the traditional pattern was for gangs working on the oldest models (the oldest 'vintages') to have the lowest earnings and those on the newest to earn most. The relatively infrequent opportunities that this provided for negotiation (they might be several years apart) were taken to raise earnings to the top of the hierarchy. A gang arguing with management over new job values would maintain that there should be sufficient 'slack' in them to allow for future inflation, especially if the new job were expected to have a long production run. Despite the bargaining strength of the labour forces concerned, very considerable inequities were tolerated under this rule. Some of the more enduring models of cars on our roads are notorious among the men who made them for the relatively low earnings that they provided. In recent years with growing inflationary pressures this pattern has weakened. To an increasing extent minor 'face-lifts' to vehicles have been taken as sufficient justification for bargaining on all job values on the model irrespective of whether the jobs have in fact altered. Thus the pattern displayed at factory C in the late 1960s would probably have been more marked in previous years.

This custom and practice rule governing the frequency of bargaining arises to a large extent from the technical fact that a new model of car introduces a wave of new jobs whereas in the other factories new jobs filter in more evenly. But it is likely that another factor contributes to this 'vintage ranking' pattern of behaviour. The bargaining behaviour of gangs is likely to differ from that of individuals for two sorts of reason. In the first place, it is a generally recognized psychological occurrence that people in groups tend to adopt more extreme positions than the same people acting as individuals. Group activity tends to reinforce and polarize attitudes and more extreme bargaining behaviour can be expected to result. Secondly, a pieceworker bargaining as an individual is probably made more aware of the established differentials of a plant than he would be as a member of a gang. As an individual there are likely to be more urgent social pressures acting on him if he were to disrupt the status quo. It would be his friends and workmates whose differentials he disrupted; the gang member's friends are likely to be within the same gang. Thus gangs are likely to use different sorts of reference group and to operate more competitively than individual pieceworkers. An example of such competitive behaviour among the fitting gangs at factory A is given later in this chapter.

This discussion has drawn out two very different patterns of bargaining behaviour. The movement of earnings under them can be compared to the movement of individual people in a crowd that is gradually moving forward. For the 'stable ranking' pattern the analogy is one of the individuals in the crowd moving in short jerks, fairly frequently but out of time with each other. When they act like this the individuals keep much the same position in the crowd with respect to one another and the whole crowd keeps a fairly constant shape as it moves forwards. By contrast, the analogy with the 'vintage ranking' pattern is one in which the individuals in the crowd move much less frequently. But when they do they do so in groups which rush to the very front only to be overtaken later by other groups coming up from behind. Under this impulse the movement of the whole crowd is uneven and its shape varies as it bunches and stretches.

Although these patterns are, to some extent, caricatures of the two extremes on a spectrum of behaviour, they provide a useful foundation on which to base a description of the internal dynamics of piecework wage structures. The example of factory C also shows how the technical nature of the work and the organizational nature of the workforce influence these dynamics.

The Sources of Differentials

The previous section cast some light upon the movement of individual earnings within a piecework pay structure but said nothing about the differentials that exist within it. Although it noted evidence of occupational differentials within single skill groups, it gave no clue either on how these come about or to what determines the scatter of earnings. It might be expected, *a priori*, that variations in individual efforts would account for much of the latter and that more subtle variations of skill than are recognized in base rates would account for the former.

EFFORT VARIATION AND WAGE SCATTER

The scatter of earnings that arises under piecework is not merely the consequence of variations between 'tight' and 'slack' job values that have arisen from the vagaries of bargaining. Whether it is because they are physically stronger or because they need the money more, some men work harder than others.

or neither.

TABLE 3:5

The scatter of earnings—the actual scatter and the scatter to be expected from relating the typical scatter of effort to the proportion of the wage that is 'variable', by factory

		A	B	C	D	E	F	G	H	J	K
Proportion of standard wage that is 'variable'	%	75	70	60	55	100	75	75	35	40	65
Actual CV of standard earnings within a single skill grade	%	25	14·5	n.a.	12	13·5	10	20	3	n.a.	n.a.
Expected CV of standard earnings	%	9	8	—	7	12	9	9	4	—	—

To assess the importance of this effect it is necessary first to have some knowledge of the natural variation in effort to be found in a typical workforce. This is available from a number of studies.[13] One of these[14] cites the results of two experiments in which groups of workers carried out tasks (in one case 'block-throwing' and in the other, particularly appropriate to this study, semi-automatic capstan lathe operation) and in both cases the scatter of the resultant distribution of output (and, by implication, effort) was Normal with a CV of between 12.0 and 12.5 per cent.

How much such a scatter of effort will influence the scatter of piecework earnings will depend upon the proportion of the wage (in terms of composition) that is variable. Although this proportion can be defined as that part of the wage which will vary with output it should be noted that, in fact, there is usually a variety of 'fall-back guarantees' that protect workers from the full range of this fluctuation. This row of Table 3:5 gives the variable proportion of the

[13] For example, R. M. Barnes, *Motion and Time Study*, Wiley, 1937, 5th ed 1963; W. C. Glassey, *The Theory and Practice of Time Study*, Business Publications Ltd, 1966; J. A. Parton, *Motion and Time Study Manual*, New York: Conover-Mast, 1952. Barnes, *op. cit.*, p. 393, says 'If the average incentive pace is 125 per cent, it is expected that the average hourly output of two thirds of all workers would fall in a range extending from 15 per cent below this point to 15 per cent above this point.' He also reports the general finding that this distribution 'would fit fairly closely to the normal bell curve'.

[14] Barnes, *op. cit.*, pp. 394–6.

wage for each factory which, it will be seen, ranges from 100 per cent for the non-federated firm through to 35 per cent.

From this it is possible to deduce the CV that one would expect a typical scatter of effort to bring to piecework earnings. This appears as the third row and can be compared with the figure in the second row which is the actual CV of earnings already presented in Table 3:1. It should be noted that in most factories studied the pieceworkers did not have obvious group restrictions of output or earnings such as were reported in the Hawthorne and other studies.

It is evident that with the sole exception of factory H the actual scatter of earnings is greater than that which would be expected from effort variations alone. The aberrant position of H undoubtedly arises from the close supervision and relatively docile labour force at the factory. Foremen are able to chivvy the slower workers into greater efforts. The experimentally derived scatter of effort was obtained in the absence of supervisory pressure.

Generally it appears to be the case that the scatter of earnings requires more than effort variation for its explanation. This is especially true of A. The experimentally derived statistic would suggest that about 90 per cent of workers' earnings should fall within 20 per cent of the average while, in fact, only 65 per cent do so.

SKILL VARIATION AS AN EXPLANATORY FACTOR

Within factories it is often freely admitted that there are marked variations in the skill of different occupations even though they are classed together for payment purposes. For the factories studied skill is, in any case, difficult to define as there is substantial in-plant training and the trade unions in the districts concerned do not have strong views about 'dilutees' (or do not make them felt). Variations in occupational skills, especially among those officially classified as 'skilled', could be an important explanatory factor behind internal piecework wage structures. The fact that differentials between sections are stable over time reinforces this hypothesis.

Discussion of skill is abominably difficult and, as Rowe says, '. . . wage theorists have little or nothing to say about the influence of skill as a differential factor in wage determination.'[15] He goes on to observe that this leads to the frustrating assumption that the only quantitative measure of a skill is its relative wage, an assumption that is frustrating because it forbids investigation of a crucial and interesting relationship. Rowe worked his way round this circularity by embarking upon a careful investigation of the changing technology in the metal trades at the turn of the century and then by testing the qualitative changes in skills that they brought against the contemporaneous developments in wages. It is of incidental interest that he found strong institutional pressures which prevented wages movements from reflecting these skill changes. More important to this discussion is the fact that he drew up a hierarchy of the skills required by the operators of different types of metal cutting machinery.

The machinery in use in the factories to be considered here is, in general, sufficiently like that being introduced in the 1920s for effective comparison. Taking account of the swing away from manual to mental skills (such as working from blueprints) Rowe drew up seven classes in order of skill and craftsmanship.[16] It was, none the less, difficult for the current study to find two comparable workshops from the sample of ten factories. This is a reflection of the considerable extent to which tools and equipment are specialized to the particular product of the factory. However, factories A and B provided neighbouring examples with

[15] J. W. F. Rowe, *Wages in Practice and Theory*, London: George Routledge and Sons, 1928, reissued 1969 by Routledge and Kegan Paul, p. 37.
[16] *ibid.* p. 98. On some occupations Rowe was wholly agnostic. Thus on Fitters he declared, 'It is hardly an exaggeration to say that there is often as much difference today between two fitters working in two shops in the same town, or even in the same shop, as between a labourer and a pattern maker.' *op. cit.*, p. 103.

very similar technology and similar quality requirements and, presumably, similar skills.

The matters requiring clarification are, first, the extent to which pay within these plants is correlated with Rowe's skill gradings and, second, how far they themselves are comparable in this respect. It was possible to obtain earnings figures for the early months of both 1969 and 1970 for certain groups of skilled machinists (mostly containing more than 20 men) for both factories. Table 3:6 shows the average of these two years' earnings figures, by factory and machine type, as percentages of their current factory averages. The differentials between section averages are substantial for factory A and have remained fairly stable. For B they are less marked and have changed rank position often over the previous decade.

TABLE 3:6

Skill categories and average earnings on different machining sections for factories A and B in comparison with Rowe

		Factory A		Factory B	
Type of machine	Rowe's skill category	earnings as % of average	rank order	earnings as % of average	rank order
grinding	1	96	4	101	3
milling	1	94	5	105	1
centre-lathes	1	82	6	103	2
capstan-lathes	2	79	7	94	4=
planing	3	98	3	—	
boring	3	104	1	—	
drilling	5	100	2	94	4=

The Table compares these earnings figures and their ranking with the ranking of skill devised by Rowe. It is immediately apparent that, although they are geographically and technically close, the two factories show a very different ranking. Further, neither of them accords well with Rowe's ranking of skill. Indeed, the more stable and marked set of statistics, that of factory A, is negatively correlated with it. They are at direct loggerheads. Although great weight cannot be attached to one piece of evidence, it does suggest that other factors are over-riding skill as determinants of earnings differentials.

There is nothing new in the observation that the rank order of the earnings on different jobs differs between factories. MacKay et al established this in broad terms[17] and Turner *et al.*[18] noted '... the extreme lack of correspondence between the hierarchical orders in which different jobs rank themselves in terms of hourly pay, as between one plant and another—or even between various plants of the same firm. ... So that a job which may in one plant be highly rated in terms of the plant's internal pay hierarchy may in another plant be lowly rated and *vice versa.*'

The term 'differential' in the context of this discussion of section or job average earnings should be qualified whenever individual pieceworkers are involved. There are no distinct differentials between sectional earnings bands in these factories; they overlap enormously. In factory A, for instance, while the CV for all pieceworkers is 25 per cent, that for most of the sections given in table 3:6 is as high as 20 per cent. But this does not prevent the individual earnings within the sections from coming from statistically distinct populations. Nor does it prevent the notion of 'sectional average earnings' having an important significance in the minds of negotiators. Nor, finally, does it weaken the impression that skill may have little influence upon earnings differentials between individual pieceworkers.

WORK STUDY PROBLEMS AND THE ORIGINS OF DIFFERENTIALS

Product technology appears to be a more satisfactory explanation of many differentials than skill. It was said earlier that the work study engineer or ratefixer is confronted with two distinct tasks. He has to decide how long the normal worker is likely to take over the job and he has to

---

[17] MacKay *et. al., op. cit.,* p. 118.
[18] H. A. Turner, G. Clack and G. Roberts, *Labour Relations in the Motor Industry,* London: George Allen and Unwin, 1967, p. 145.

decide what level of earnings that worker 'ought' in some sense to get from it. The accuracy with which he can do the first of these depends to a large extent upon the job technology; some jobs are much harder to work study than others. On such jobs it is easier for the pieceworker to confuse his bargaining opponent and get earnings higher than the work study engineer expects.

Certain jobs are anathema to work study engineers. Although piecework wage structures vary considerably between establishments there are some jobs which regularly crop up with relatively high earnings even though the plants in which they occur have very different technologies. A polisher, for instance, presses the part he is working on against a revolving buff and the speed with which he achieves the required finish depends upon the pressure that he applies. During the work study it is easy for the man being timed to appear to press harder than he does in fact and, once a job value has been awarded, he can exploit the slack job value. Polishers were the highest earning groups at factories B and K. Straighteners had high earnings at F and G for two reasons. In the first place technical improvements in the tubes and bars with which they worked had, over many years, diminished the task of straightening. Second, and more important, the operation itself (in which the tube is spun between centres and eccentricities registered on a dial so that deft use of a hammer can tap them out) is all but impossible to work study. Much the same applies to wheel balancers (at F and G) and tinsmiths (at C). Spring adjusters (at D) feel the tension of the metal in their finger tips with a sensitivity which no watching work study engineer can assess. An experienced grinder (at B, G and F) can raise an impressive spray of sparks while barely touching the metal he is supposed to be cutting. The anomalous earnings levels that arise from technical work study problems such as these tend to be treated fatalistically by work study engineers and by other workers alike. Sometimes they are unconvincingly rationalized as being reflections of subtle skills. More often they are joked about as 'just their luck'.

Conversely, of course, jobs which are easy to work study tend to have below average earnings. Generally, ease of work study appears to account for a high proportion of stable differentials. It has already been noted that factory A has its pattern of differentials (insofar as they exist) inverted with respect to skill. Part of the explanation comes from the extent to which the machines have the cutting operation automatically controlled. For capstan lathes (where average earnings were 79 per cent of factory average) 85 per cent of the time taken over a job was completely controlled by the machine. For drilling, on the other hand, (with average earnings at 100 per cent of factory average) the characteristics of the product meant that only 30 per cent of the job time was predetermined machine time. The rest of the job was spent setting up and adjusting the work: activities where there is vast scope for mystifying the ratefixer. Another part of the explanation of A's differentials lies in the length of the job. The jobs that were (on Rowe's classification) less skilled, drilling and boring, were more concentrated on big castings and took very much longer than the more skilled ones. As one foreman put it, 'to measure these jobs you don't want a stop watch so much as a calendar'. In A a long job provided much more leeway for the pieceworker.

The precise way in which the technical characteristics influence earnings depends to some extent upon the prevailing custom and practice rules of the establishment. For instance, at B the drillers' earnings were exceptionally low because most of their work was in short batches while the fitters earned the highest because their work batches were large. Here the allowances paid for changing jobs and setting up machines were relatively meagre and the ratefixers were permitted (by management and custom and practice) to be more precise in their procedures than at A. Hence high earnings came from the short-cuts and 'learning curve' improvements that showed up on a long run on the same job.

In factory E, on the other hand, the custom and practice was that men padded out their earnings on the generously paid 'interference time' and the pieceworkers who earned far and away the highest were not the more skilled grinders but the automatic machine operators. Their machines were slow to set up—in some cases 75 per cent of allowed time was setting time—and by completing this well within the period that they had persuaded the work study engineer was necessary they pushed up their pay.

So far this discussion has examined explanations of the differentials that occur in piecework wage structures in terms of technical attributes: effort variation, skill and the weaknesses of work study. The first and third of these factors contribute part of an explanation but do not tell us why differentials sometimes change, and they are mostly of relevance to the first of the ratefixer's tasks, that of estimating how long a job will take. They contribute nothing to an understanding of what level of earnings will be considered to be 'fair' in argument over comparability.

The Use of Comparisons

Whatever the paraphernalia and precision of work study, in all but the most docile of workforces the pieceworker and his management opponent are going to have to bargain about the level of earnings that they think 'ought' to be earned. Their argument will revolve around comparisons. The use of wage comparisons by bargainers raises two distinct issues. The first is that of the information on wages that they possess. If the worker has information on a potentially favourable comparison it is likely, if he believes it to be true, to influence his expectations. If he can persuade his management opponent that it is true, it is likely to influence the bargain directly. The second issue is concerned with the group with whom the comparison is being made. The management opponent is unlikely to pay attention to the comparison unless the worker can persuade him that the group concerned is a legitimate comparative reference group for the worker.

THE AVAILABILITY OF EARNINGS INFORMATION

There are three broad sources of comparison which piece-workers might use: earnings in other factories, earnings of timeworkers in their own factories, and earnings of other pieceworkers in their own factories.

It is very difficult to evaluate the impact of earnings information from outside the plant. Generally, people appear to know relatively little about earnings in other factories and the scatter of individual piecework earnings makes them difficult to interpret. Although both employers and unions often have accurate and comprehensive information about time-rate earnings in other plants, these are rarely if ever brought into piecework bargains. Some of the better publicized measured-daywork agreements in engineering are sometimes used and, in Coventry, the now defunct Toolroom Rate was widely used in the factories with lower earnings levels. The nationally publicized pay negotiations in other industries probably have the same nebulous impact upon bargainers as do impressions about rises in the cost of living.

So far as comparisons with timeworkers within the factory are concerned, the information is readily available to piece-workers. Generally it seems safe to say that, while timerates are affected to a substantial extent by increases in piece-work earnings, the reverse is not the case. Inside the factory as outside, pieceworkers rarely if ever make comparisons with timeworkers' rates. It is comparisons with fellow piece-workers within the factory which appear to be most important. But the scope for this is restricted both by the amount of information collected by management and by the amount that it makes available to the workers.

Of course, all workers have some knowledge of the earnings of their workmates but, given all the complications of different hours of work, different tax codes and the like, this knowledge is likely to be impressionistic and unreliable. Earnings surveys by shop stewards themselves are rare for, not surprisingly, they find it difficult to obtain data systematically. They consequently tend to depend upon management for earnings information. In most of the factories covered in this study, management's own knowledge of earnings was very incomplete. In some cases data were collected for a specific purpose. For instance, some of the Coventry plants were obliged to collect standard earnings data for the compilation of the Coventry Toolroom Rate. Another instance is provided by factory F which was obliged to calculate the factory average standard hourly earnings in order to calculate the indirect workers' lieu bonus. Some plants calculated sectional averages of standard earnings; others calculated only average percentage bonus levels.

Most junior managers and ratefixers had access to the best data that management possessed, although they often did not make use of it. But in many establishments, notably D, H, J and K, managers were forbidden from passing any of this information on to workers. At the other extreme the data were available to shop stewards on request or were, as at F, pinned on the notice boards. Between these extremes there were unofficial arrangements whereby stewards could find out the average earnings of their own sections. Workers generally have most information about earning in high Topsy factories.

A GENETIC ANALOGY

At this stage of the argument it is relevant to bring forward and test a very simple model of the bargaining process. An hypothesis of genetic evolution was proposed by Fisher in 1930 that suggested that 'the rate of increase of fitness of any species is equal to the genetic variation of fitness.'[19] By analogy, the greater the scatter of earnings is within an individual piecework system then, for a given frequency of bargain, the more extravagant is the range of earnings with which any individual pieceworker can make comparison and, it might be hypothesized, the greater the rate of non-

[19] quoted by K. F. Dyer, *New Scientist*, 22 August 1968.

negotiated drift that will result. Even with the 'stable ranking' pattern of bargaining, a larger scatter of earnings will
mean a larger gap between the earnings of any individual
and those of his neighbours in the rank order. Consequently, one would expect a correlation between the Topsy
factor and the scatter of individual earnings by factory.

One difficulty confronting the testing of this is the fact that
high Topsy firms tend to have a wage composition with a
high variable component. In fact, however, this common
factor proves to be inadequate to account for the relatively
high correlation ($R^2 = 0.81$) between the CV of earnings
and the Topsy factor. The data certainly support the
hypothesis although, as the next chapter will demonstrate,
there are other reasons why one might expect the relationship to hold. Whatever other factors are at work, it seems
safe to conclude that a wide scatter of piecework earnings
will be a contributory factor behind non-negotiated drift.

WHAT MAKES COMPARISONS EFFECTIVE

However good the earnings information is, there are strong
pressures for the individual pieceworker's earnings not to
move too far from their traditional rank position. There
are pressures on the individual from his fellow workers
not to 'push things too far' and also from the need to pre-
severve a tolerable bargaining relationship with his foreman and ratefixer. On the ratefixer there are more or less
strong management controls obliging him to keep the individual's earnings broadly 'in line'. The earlier statistical
analysis showed the resulting wage structure to be remark-
ably stable.

The stability of wage differentials over time has been
noted by several authors. Rowe commented that 'a cursory
examination of the problem of wage differentials . . . strongly
emphasizes the far-reaching effects of sheer custom, and its
domination over men's minds. . . . We do not realize the
little changes in everyday life which sap the logical foundations of our ideas, and custom has time to consolidate the
structure before those foundations have completely crumb-

led.'[20] Wootton noted that 'It is not ... surprising that ...
history should be summoned to fill the void when moral
actions must be performed without moral principles to guide
them.'[21]

There are great advantages to the negotiators in sticking
to traditional comparisons and generally prevailing wage
increases. Ross observes that 'there is an additional reason
why going rates and going increases are likely to be followed.
The ready-made settlement supplies an answer, a solution,
a formula. It is mutually face-saving. ... It is the one settlement which permits both parties to believe they have done
a proper job, the one settlement which has the best chance
of being "sold" to the company's board of directors and the
union's rank and file.'[22]

It would be very wrong, however, to conclude that all
piecework bargaining is a matter of placid consensus.
Changes are continually taking place within the pay structure which alert pieceworkers are likely to use to their bargaining advantage. An illustration can be taken
from a factory (not one of the main ten case studies)[23]
which introduced among its existing production lines a process called 'sintering' whereby components are pressed out of
metal powder instead of being machined from castings in
the traditional way. Because it was a new technology there
were a number of 'teething troubles' which gave rise to
relatively slack piecework times. The pieceworkers concerned
saw their earnings rise ten per cent above those of sections
with which they had previously had parity. Because the
technique was new, and also because the product being
made by it was unique to the section, this differential was
accepted by the workforce as a whole and it remained un-

---

[20] Rowe, *op. cit.*, p. 111. A similar discussion is to be found in
Doeringer and Piore, *op. cit.*, p. 40.

[21] B. Wootton, *The Social Foundations of Wage Policy*, London:
Unwin University Books, 1962 edn, p. 162.

[22] A. M. Ross, *Trade Union Wage Policy*, Berkeley: University of
California, 1956, p. 52.

[23] J. M. Kidd, unpublished MA thesis, University of Warwick,
1969.

disturbed for two years. At this point management introduced some products onto the sintering line which were already being made on established lines by conventional techniques. This similarity of product was immediately taken by workers on the established lines as a justification for making comparison with the sinterers. Although the labour force was largely one of women who had rarely taken collective action against management, the other sections were able to raise their earnings sharply. After a brief attempt by the sinterers to reassert the differential it vanished forever.

This example illustrates how workers can accept an earnings differential if there is a clear technical distinction between themselves and the group concerned. But once an obvious common factor links their own membership reference group with the other group, thus making it an apparently legitimate comparative reference group, the pressures for parity may start. It is not only technical distinctions that can insulate groups from mutual comparison. There are organizational factors such as, for instance, occurred in factory B where two merged companies operated in the same building. Workers next to each other tolerated a differential for many years until eventually the managements were fully merged and the differential had to be hastily negotiated away. Similarly, workers can tolerate surprisingly wide differentials between those working on similar jobs if they are in separate parts of the factory.

It is very difficult, however, to predict what sort of a change, technical, organizational or otherwise, will cause workers to seize upon a new comparative reference group and persuade junior management of its legitimacy. The use of reference group concepts is in any case made difficult by the scatter of piecework earnings. For instance, a pieceworker on a milling machine section may be used to earning ten per cent above the average of his section. If he discovers that the neighbouring capstan lathe section has average earnings ten per cent above those of his own, will he feel aggrieved and press for more? The answer to this is likely to lie in what might be called the political condition of the workforce.

SHOP STEWARD CONTROL OF COMPARISONS

Chapter Five will be concerned with the political processes operating in the course of piecework bargaining. For the moment attention will be paid only to the impact of these upon the formation of reference groups. An interesting light is cast upon this question by the American sociologists Lipset and Trow[24] in their consideration of nation-wide trade union behaviour. They note that 'which reference groups individuals use, and how they use them, are questions intimately related to their feelings regarding the *rightness*, the legitimacy of the comparisons made.'[25] They argue that political leaders tend to reinforce their position by attempting to establish 'a sense of pertinent similarity' between one group and another and that this causes reference groups to spread. 'As part of the struggle for power among competing leadership groups their manipulations of comparisons tend to emphasize the importance of general status categories as over against the spontaneous use of face to face intimates as comparative references. It is a short step from the observation to the hypothesis that *the more active the political life of a union*, and the more *factional and competitive* is the propaganda to which the rank and file is exposed, the more membership will tend to appraise comparatively its own wages and working conditions on the basis of general status categories.'[26]

Much of this could probably be transferred straight to the piecework shop. The growth of what Chapter Five will call the 'bargaining awareness' of a workforce is likely to be accompanied by, first, reference groups crystallizing. A workforce that is fairly naïve in bargaining and takes most

[24] S. Lipset and M. Trow, 'Reference Group Theory and Trade Union Wage Policy', in M. Komarovsky, *Common Frontiers of the Social Sciences,* Glencoe: Free Press, 1957.

[25] *ibid.,* p. 403.

[26] *ibid.,* p. 405.

management actions for granted is likely to consist of workers with only dim impressions of what others earn and vague feelings that 'there must be a good reason' for differentials that exist. With the questioning of this and with the first stirrings of some sort of work group collective action, workers are likely to look for uniformity within work groups and possibly question differentials between them. The development of the shop steward system and the gradual 'integration' of the workforce as a political unit will tend to further this process and make membership reference groups coalesce.

But it would be wrong to conclude that the development of shopfloor bargaining leads to the elimination of all differentials. As has been observed, they can persist for very long periods. It appears that shop steward activity can be an important factor in assisting this. An illustration of this comes from Factory G which has a heavily bargained piecework system and strong shop stewards' committee. The whole factory is devoted to the production of a single component in a wide range of dimensions. In 1961 a new product was introduced which fulfilled a similar mechanical function to the major product but incorporated a radically different engineering technique. There was heavy pressure from the customers to expand production of the innovation and, in the general confusion, 'slack' piecework values were placed on jobs connected with it. Consequently, by the end of the year earnings of those working on the new product had risen 12 per cent above the average of the old product sections. By the end of 1962 the differential was 22 per cent. Over the next five years (and, so far as the writer knows, longer) this differential remained between 22 and 26 per cent despite the fact that all jobs were reobserved or changed many times over the period. Although there was no difference in the nature of the semi-skilled jobs at which the men worked on the different products, and although they worked under the same roof, both management and the senior stewards said that comparisons between them 'just aren't made'. If they were made, it was said, they were ruled out as inapplicable. Even though the aberrant differential had arisen through a management error the shop stewards' committee accepted it and actively prevented comparison. The reason for this action, it appears, lies in the committee's concern to preserve its 'bargaining relationship' with management—a concept to which Chapter Five will pay more attention. The cost to management of removing the differential would be so great that the committee was content not to 'push things too far' by pressing for it.

The wisdom of this action is demonstrated by an example from factory A, whose workforce was quite as willing to take strike action as that at G but whose shop steward committee was weak and where the degree of political integration was low. The misrecording of waiting time in the factory increased over the late 1960s, especially among the four gangs of fitters who made up one quarter of the direct labour force. These gangs tended to compete in earnings among themselves and they tended to keep gang earnings close together. The average earnings of all four gangs had been above those of other piecework groups in the factory for at least fifteen years. Over the 1960s they maintained their average earnings between 5 and 10 per cent above the average for the whole factory. In 1970, however, the misrecording of waiting time by the fitters got out of hand. In a sort of 'normative breakdown' the competing gangs drove each other to misrecord more and more. The spiralling of earnings that resulted drove the fitters' average earnings for 1970 to 25 per cent above the factory average. This flagrant exploiting of the system forced a hitherto tolerant management to intervene. It froze their earnings unilaterally and, when the fitters came out on strike for several weeks, the rest of the factory refused to join them. The political integration of the workforce had been inadequate to prevent this cumulative competition among the fitters and it was clear that the workforce resented the breach with management that had been brought about. With good reason: largely as a consequence of these events management embarked upon the replacement of the whole piecework system.

There is another way in which what might broadly be

called the political maturity of the workforce impinges upon internal wage structures. Especially in factories with relatively docile workforces, it is common for certain sections to have higher earnings than others simply because they have a higher propensity to bargain. Typically, at D a ratefixer commented 'the machine room are an awkward lot; they argue about everything'. Similar aberrations were evident at factories E and H. Interestingly this phenomenon of a favourable differential arising apparently solely from the high bargaining propensity of a section was most noticeable in low Topsy factories. In the high Topsy ones bargaining propensity was much more uniform and is less likely to account for the existence of differentials.

An exception which illustrates this is provided by factory B where differentials between section average earnings had remained fairly constant for at least ten years. The grinding section had always had the highest average earnings. In 1968, however, the grinders toppled to the fourth position among the six major sections. From remaining steadily between 10 and 15 per cent above the factory average, its average earnings fell to just below the factory average. There was, in part, a technical reason for this in that there were shortages of work for a time. But this is not a sufficient explanation, for other sections experienced work shortages without such serious or prolonged consequences for their earnings. This uncommonly marked change in the internal wage structure was accompanied by another unusual event. The minutes of the shop steward committee show the senior stewards pressing the grinding section to fill its vacancy for a shop steward. Eventually the committee decided to warn the grinders that, unless they put forward a shop steward of their own the main committee would make no efforts on their behalf on any matters. The absence of a steward on the section appeared to be a reflection of the weak bargaining propensity of the section at that time. When eventually a steward was elected in 1970 the traditional position of the grinders at the top of the league table was restored, partly through increased bargaining pressure by the indi-

vidual workers and partly through a formal bargain with
management (negotiated wage drift). This episode suggests
that sections of pieceworkers can sometimes fall from their
traditional position in the internal wage structure through
bargaining inactivity. It also suggests that an integrated
shop steward committee can take active steps to prevent this.

Wage differentials have such obvious importance for a
workforce that it is inevitable that they should be influenced
by the political activity of workers. These illustrations show
that the way in which they are influenced is not at all simple.
On the one hand, the more a workforce tends to bargain
over its piecework values, the more it is likely to become
conscious of comparative reference groups and the more
individual workers are likely to question the legitimacy of
many differentials. On the other hand, as the workforce
becomes more politically integrated through a shop steward
body, the stewards may act to preserve certain differentials.
A closer analysis of shop steward motivations and how these
influence the processes at work must be left until Chapter
Five.

*   *   *

This chapter has attempted to describe in statistical terms
how individual piecework wages move with respect to each
other. It also explored the extent to which effort, skill and
technical variations account for this. The use of comparisons by bargainers has now been considered. But this still
does not add up to a satisfactory analysis of the bargaining
process and it cannot be satisfactory until the question of
power has been considered. The next three chapters are
concerned with the determinants of a pieceworker's bargaining power.

4

The 'Custom and Practice' Rules

In any piecework system, bargaining takes place within a framework of widely acknowledged rules. The more important of these rules cover procedural matters such as which individuals are entitled to reach an agreement on a job value, under what circumstances a job may be revalued, and what form of work study procedure the management representative may use. Others may appear substantive at first sight but they have strong procedural implications. Examples of these are the rate at which a pieceworker will be paid when his job is in dispute and the amount of control he may have over the speed of work while his job is being work-studied. More than anything else, the content of these rules expresses the relative power of the bargainers. The rules are the major determinants of whether the outcome of a particular bargain will be favourable to management or to the worker.

This chapter is concerned with the nature of these rules and with their effect upon the bargain. Are they merely the superficial reflections of profounder forces or do they deserve to be considered serious determinants in their own right? If they do affect the power relationship between the shopfloor bargainers, is this reflected in the Topsy factors of the factories studied?

The Nature of 'Custom and Practice' Rules[1]

Like any other aspect of human activity, workshop

[1] A detailed discussion of custom and practice and particularly of the way in which it is legitimized is to be found in W. A. Brown,

behaviour is replete with regular patterns. People act repeti-
tively through habit, through custom, because it is the best
way of getting things done, and because the social pressure
of a convention makes it best to act that way. But in the
context of collective bargaining the patterns of behaviour
that are particularly interesting are those that govern the
reciprocal relationships between management and workers.
These have some of the support of social sanctions that
conventions enjoy but they also have some of the legitimacy
of a legal contract between two people. They can be best
described as 'transactional rules'.

A strict definition of a transactional rule would be that it
is a pattern of behaviour governed by a reciprocity relationship between two parties which both parties regard as legitimate.[2] The transactional rules of job regulation were classified by Flanders[3] according to their authorship. In the
context of piecework there are two obvious sources of rules.
These are the unilateral edicts of management and the
collective agreements between management and workers.
Many piecework systems were initially introduced by
management in an atmosphere where negotiation was un-
necessary. What little negotiation did take place was probably
over no more than the earnings increase that should accompany the innovation and possibly over such matters as
the disputes procedure to be followed in the event of a failure
to agree over a job value. Most of the factories involved in
this study had carried out their last major overhaul of their

---

'A Consideration of "Custom and Practice" ', *British Journal of
Industrial Relations*, March 1972. An interestingly different analysis
of the term is given in M. Rimmer, *Race and Industrial Conflict*,
Warwick Studies in Industrial Relations, London: Heinemann
Educational Books, 1972, which includes a description of the impact
upon C&P rules of a normative breakdown resulting from racial
conflict.

[2] F. Barth, *Models of Social Organisation*, Royal Anthropological
Institute Occasional Paper, No 23, 1966, pp. 1–11, discusses transactional relationships at length in the context of a Scandinavian
fishing fleet.

[3] A. Flanders, *Industrial Relations: What is Wrong with the System?*,
London: Faber, 1965, p. 9.

Key to the table on the comparison of C&P drift in ten factories

Index rating

See 32pp.
Tr

Criterion for job reobservation
1. None for other than 'material, means or method'.
2. General management control over reobservations on systematic basis.
3. Time limit on age of job.
4. Level of earnings related to neighbours; some requests refused.
5. 'Bad' jobs; effectively on demand.

Compensation for mobility between jobs
1. None; solely management discretion.
2. 'Learning curve' allowed if moved as favour to management.
3. Made up to average if a favour to management; otherwise loss.
4. Made up fully to average in most circumstances.
5. Full and immediate compensation for earnings loss.

Operator control of 'feeds and speeds' of machines
1. None.
3. Some control, connived at by foremen.
5. Extensive; management having little effective control.

Waiting time payment for machine breakdowns
1. Less than or equal to 80 per cent of average earnings.
2. Less than or equal to 90 per cent of average earnings.
3. Over-recorded or avoided often.
4. Usually over-recorded to give average earnings.
5. Always guaranteed average earnings.

Payment when no piecework value is available
1. Less than or equal to 90 per cent.
3. Paid retrospectively, misrecorded or 'unofficially' compensated.
5. Always guaranteed average earnings.

Restrictions on work study engineers or ratefixers
1. Strict work study well supported by foremen.
2. Stop watches permitted but allowances bargained over extensively.
3. No stop watches but effort rating and method study.
4. Some timing permitted but study cursory and little foreman support.
5. Pure 'Persian market' bargain, no effort rating and foremen unhelpful.

E

The only way to test this hypothesis is to look at the evidence. For this the transactional rules covering six areas of the piecework bargain were taken for the ten factories studied. They were compared on a simple five point scale. This ranged from one point, for the end of the spectrum associated with strict rules that had not drifted, through to five points for the worker-generous or 'lenient' rules that had drifted a long way. Apart from most of the rules rated '1' or '2', all these rules were, in fact, of C&P origin.

The key to Table 4:1 shows the different stages of the rules on each topic. It takes no more than a superficial look at them to see that the scales are crude and, in many cases, vague. But since they are not intended to establish a refined point they are sufficient for the purpose. Similarly, whilst the rating given to each factory is precise in most instances, it is less so in some because of the diversity of C&P within those factories. What this simple effort at quantification does show fairly convincingly is that individual factories are generally consistent in their rating on the scale right across all six rule areas. Their mean deviation from the mean (a measure of their internal consistency) is on average only half a point on the scale.

Since there is little doubt that the rules have reached their position on the scale (apart from those with 1 or 2 points) through the process of C&P drift described in this chapter, it seems reasonable to conclude that, at least in the context of piecework systems, C&P does drift on a broad front.

The consequences for non-negotiated drift

This analysis of the C&P rules of piecework has emphasized the impact that they have upon the relative bargaining power of the ratefixer and pieceworker. The further C&P drifts, the stronger it makes the pieceworker at the ratefixer's expense. Consider, for example, the position of a pieceworker confronted with precise work study and a financial penalty for failing to agree. Compare his position with that of another pieceworker at another factory bargaining with a ratefixer who can only use a wristwatch and knows that a failure to agree will not affect the pieceworker's pay packet. The bargain is likely to yield a greater increase in earnings for the second man than for the first.

It should be noted that lenient C&P rules increase the bargaining power of the *individual* pieceworker. They do not necessarily have the same effect upon the bargaining power of the whole workforce. That is a matter to be considered in the next chapter. But because it is the individual bargain that is affected one would expect it to be non-negotiated wage drift that shows this effect. Put simply, is non-negotiated wage drift a function of the leniency of C&P rules?

Table 4:1 shows, for each of the ten factories, an index of how far the C&P rules have drifted in six key areas connected with the piecework bargain. It also shows, as a simple average of these, an index of 'C&P leniency' for each factory. Although this is obviously a very crude indicator it can be treated with some confidence because the mean deviation from the mean of the six individual indices for each plant is small. The index of C&P leniency therefore is a useful measure of the state of C&P rules in a factory.[11]

[11] With this measure it is possible to test for other properties of C&P. One relationship that might be expected is that between the length of service of the labour force and the C&P leniency index. It could be argued that a stable labour force led to stable C&P—or, on the contrary, that only a stable labour force would have the power to consolidate C&P drift. Data were available for six of the factories but no significant relationship could be detected between C&P leniency on the one hand and average length of service and the percentage of the labour force with more than five and ten years service on the other. It may be that the factories were too much alike in this respect (their average lengths of service were between six and twelve years) for a relationship to be detected.

Another relationship that is of interest is that between C&P leniency and the scatter of earnings. The correlation coefficient between the index and the figure for the CV of individual piecework earnings given in Table 3:1 was, for the eleven firms for which there were data, 0·90. This suggests that more lenient C&P rules are associated with a greater scatter of individual earnings. It also

With both variables quantified it is now possible to test for a relationship between non-negotiated drift and C&P leniency.[12] The qualifications about the wage data that were made in Chapter Two must be re-emphasized. Although they are drawn from slightly different periods, this is unlikely to influence seriously the relationship being tested. The relationship is given in two scatter diagrams, Diagram 4:1 relating C&P leniency to the Topsy factor by plant and Diagram 4:2 relating it to the figure for the annual compound rate of non-negotiated drift by plant.

It will be seen that there is a strong relationship in each case. The correlation coefficients between the variables is, respectively for each diagram, 0.94 and 0.95 and they are significant at the 99 per cent level. The apparent neatness of this confirmation of the hypothesis should be treated with great caution. The quantification of the variables has been distinctly crude in several respects and the margin of error

---

weakens the significance of the relationship between the CV of earnings and the Topsy factor in the 'genetic analogy' discussed in the previous chapter.

[12] At the end of Chapter 2 it was noted that factories where pieceworkers reap above average 'windfall' gains from technical innovations (without 'improving' their labour input) tend also to be the factories where they are getting above average earnings increases from other sources (notably by bargaining pressure). The reason for this association should now be clear. For C&P rules will have drifted not only on those areas of the bargain that enhance the individual worker's bargaining power; they will also, elsewhere on the 'broad front', have drifted to absorb 'windfall' gains. For example, C&P rules can develop which spell out specific arrangements whereby increases in productivity resulting from technical innovation should be 'shared' between management and men. One factory, for instance, had a C&P rule between ratefixers and men that, if an innovation reduced the number of men in a gang, those remaining should share out the notional bonus earnings of the missing men and management should be entitled to any 'overhead' savings. The importance of this sort of C&P rule to the current discussion is that technical change is incorporated in both the measures used in a compatible way. For, on the one hand, both the rate of non-negotiated drift and Topsy include 'windfall' gains to pieceworkers; on the other hand, rules that determine how much pieceworkers should benefit from 'windfall' gains will be reflected in the index of C&P leniency.

DIAGRAM 4 : 1

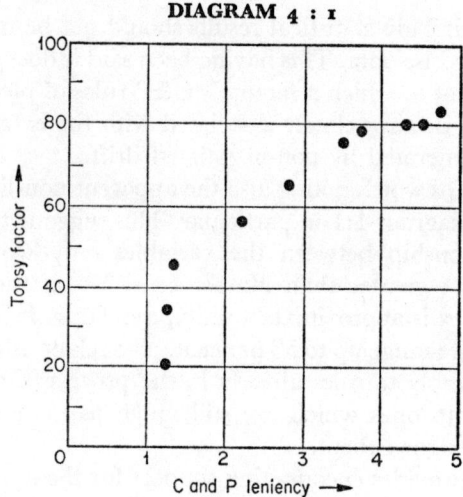

DIAGRAM 4 : 2

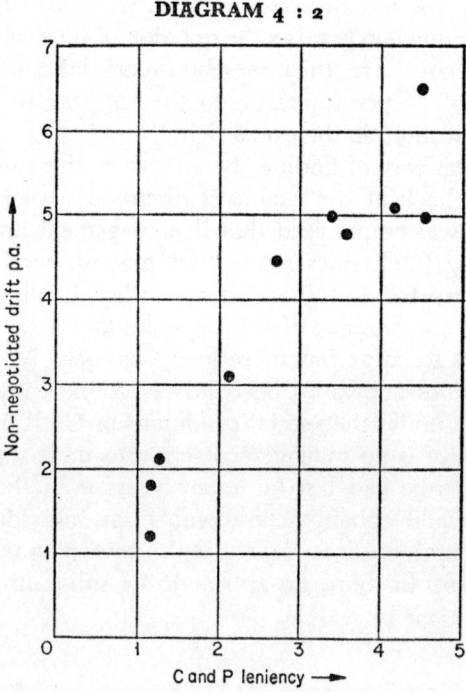

is substantial. Tidy statistical results should not be made to conceal imprecise data. This having been said it does appear that the extent to which a factory's C&P rules of piecework have drifted is fairly closely associated with the extent that wages are generated by non-negotiated drift.

It is perhaps worth noting also the apparent non-linearity evident in Diagram 4:1 in particular. This suggests that the linear relationship between the variables only works for Topsy factors greater than 50 per cent. When the C&P leniency index is approximately unity, the Topsy factor can occupy a large range up to 50 per cent. The relationship thus appears to apply to rules already in the process of drifting rather than to ones which are still much as management originally designed them.

This test provides encouraging support for the hypothesis that C&P rules governing piecework are major causal factors determining the rate of non-negotiated wage drift in a factory. This immediately raises the question of how substantial these rules are. Are they merely superficial and fragile reflections of deeper forces or do they appear to be substantial institutions in their own right?

The easiest way of finding the answer to this question is by looking back at the examples discussed earlier in this chapter. It was emphasized that if management attempted to make the C&P rules more strict towards workers this would be resisted but that, on the other hand, workers respected the legitimacy of existing rules and generally did not attempt to carve out more generous ones. As a result the C&P rules appear to be relatively stable entities that only change under the special conditions of C&P drift outlined. If there is no management error to undermine it, a given C&P rule can last for many years even though its alteration could enhance considerably the individual bargaining strength of pieceworkers. Rules governing the piecework bargain, in short, do appear to be substantial determinants in their own right.

5

The Role of Shop Stewards

SHOP STEWARDS AND THE CONTROL OF PIECEWORK WAGES

Piecework appears to be unpopular with many shop stewards. The NBPI report on PBR observed that 'We have . . . found considerable disenchantment among workers with the constant time-consuming process of shop-floor haggling, inequity, falsification of work records, inversion of customary differentials and lack of security, which are so often associated with conventional PBR systems. . . . Our investigations have shown that workers are as concerned with the equity and stability of earnings as they are with their absolute amount. . .'[1] The study found several instances where shop steward initiatives had led to conventional piecework systems being replaced by some form of timerate scheme.

The survey conducted for the Royal Commission came up with data to support this. It found that, of those stewards who had the bulk of their members on PBR, 55 per cent were in favour of replacing the system[2]. The principal reasons they gave for this antipathy were that

[1] National Board for Prices and Incomes, Report 65, *Payment by Results*, Cmnd 3627, London: HMSO, 1968, para 98.

[2] Government Social Survey, *Workplace Industrial Relations*, SS402, London: HMSO, 1968, p. 36. Conversely, 45 per cent of stewards with all or most of their members on PBR were against replacing it with another method of payment. Similar evidence of steward antipathy to PBR is given for the North-East shipbuilding industry by J. Cousins, ' . . . the piecework system cannot be said to have been popular; and it was marginally less popular among the stewards than their men.', 'The Non-militant Shop Steward', *New Society*, 3rd Feb 1972.

bonus earnings fluctuated and that they led to inequalities which 'splits up the men'. By contrast, of those stewards with a minority or none of their members on PBR, 69 per cent were opposed to changing to it. This dislike of PBR was very much less among ordinary union members: 'Of those who were paid by results, one-third were in favour of replacing this system by timerates. Of those paid by some other method and who said that it would be possible for them to be paid by results, about one-half would be in favour of changing their present system of payment.'[3] The survey concluded that 'Stewards generally seemed keener to replace payment by results than did either managment or union members.'[4]

The comments of the senior stewards at the factories involved in the current study are wholly consistent with these findings. At most of the factories with heavily bargained piecework systems there were unsolicited comments of dissatisfaction. At A the senior stewards all agreed with the one of them who called piecework a 'dog-eat-dog rat-race' that was 'vicious' in driving and dividing the men. At E they said they would gladly accept the replacement of the system with timerates despite the diminution of their power that it would bring about. Piecework was called a 'vicious, pernicious system' and the 'biggest evil in the factory' by the convenor at B. To his counterpart at F 'It is a jungle on both sides . . . on numerous occasions in an effort to get a model that is popular they (i.e. management) have been prepared to pay and therefore create an anomaly for another section and this is fatal; it is fatal for both sides. On the other hand a dying model, a car being faded out, workers on that section, say they are on eight shillings an hour, the other section where they want to get the job rolling will be paid ten or perhaps eleven shillings per hour and . . . this creates an anomaly you see. This is the position we have been in with piecework.'

To say that shop stewards tend to find piecework

[3] Government Social Survey, *op. cit.*, p. 126.
[4] *ibid.*, p. 6.

obnoxious does not necessarily imply that they are willing to change to the alternative pay system that management might propose. There are so many uncertainties for piece-workers involved in changing pay systems that they are naturally wary of it.[5] But it does suggest that stewards find unwelcome the role into which piecework forces them, despite the apparent fact that it gives them greater power and greater scope for bargaining.

One reason for this may be that a steward's job is gener-ally more time consuming under piecework than under timework. Even though most shop steward committees compensate for bonus lost during representative duties, this is often inadequate (largely, on the partial evidence of this study, because stewards put in inadequate claims for themselves). The extent to which the steward is involved in piecework bargaining varies between factories. In some they are involved in all bargains, even, in some documented cases, to the exclusion of the operator directly involved. In those covered in this study, however, it was more common for the steward to be brought in only in the event of a dis-pute between the operator and his management opponent. In the more docile factories (notably H and K) this rarely happened because the operators tended to be com-pliant. Even in some plants with aggressive work forces (for instance A) stewards were rarely brought into the bargain.

The nature of their involvement was described by the NBPI. 'Management and foremen generally thought that stewards had a moderating influence on their members in bargaining over PBR values, so that in our case studies of conventional PBR systems, shop stewards usually appear as a force for stability.' Despite suspicions expressed by some managers that a high rate of wage drift was the consequence of a deliberate strategy on the part of senior stewards, the NBPI report found no evidence in support 'nor did we find

[5] For a discussion of the problems involved in changing pay systems, see W. A. Brown, 'Changing wage payment systems', in S. Kessler and B. Weekes, *Conflict at Work*, London: BBC, 1971.

much evidence that stewards were deliberately exploiting the propensity of PBR systems to drift'.[6] Instead, the report found that stewards tended to moderate claims for outrageously high job values and, in several cases, used their control over earnings 'primarily to iron out fluctuations in week to week payment levels.'[7]

Some, though not all, of the factories involved in this study bore this out. At those where stewards played an active part in sorting out disagreements between pieceworkers and ratefixers (or foremen) they tended to prevent men 'going too far', in the words of the convenor at F. He said that his stewards 'definitely try to prevent men fiddling high earnings' or else the system would degenerate into a 'rat race'. At B the convenor described how he would often warn an inexperienced ratefixer that some particular pieceworker was 'out for all he can get' and, if the man is pushing too hard, the ratefixer walks tactfully away while the convenor 'educates' the man, threatening to 'leave him on his own if he doesn't see sense'. His successor said that if he told a worker that he was being unreasonable over a job value there would be no more argument on the matter; men could not be allowed 'to get away with murder'. This role of stewards was widely appreciated by foremen and ratefixers at several of the factories studied. They said that stewards could handle awkward individuals in a way that they themselves could not.

Further illustrations of this come from the minute book of the shop stewards' committee at B:

> The Convenor stated that an operator on the grinding section was insisting on a retime for a 17 minute operation which he could do in 5 minutes. The convenor had bluffed the ratefixer into giving another 3 minutes but the point was that the operator was being unfair in his demands

[6] NBPI, *op. cit.*, p. 180.

[7] *ibid.*, p. 94. An interesting account of an unusually sophisticated system of piecework wage control is given in S. W. Lerner, J. R. Cable and S. Gupta, *Workshop Wage Determination*, London: Pergamon, 1969, p. 90.

and had it come to a retime the operator would probably have had the time of 17 minutes cut instead of increased.

With recent redundancies of the Fitting section a member of the department had earned 28 hours in 2 hours actual time. The convenor had met the department along with its shop steward who was disgusted by this state of affairs and warned them that unless they disciplined themselves until the work position became more clarified it could easily result in further redundancies.

But by themselves these quotations are misleading. The stewards' role is not solely one of damping down the bargaining zeal of individuals. The same minute book provides evidence that over a period of at least twenty years the stewards have followed a concerted policy of pulling into line men who accept 'tight' job values and thus jeopardise the possible future earnings of their workmates.

The convenor had approached an operator on the milling section over the times he was accepting from the ratefixing department. It appeared that the operator had unwittingly allowed the ratefixer to give him the bare minimum with him operating at top feeds and speeds. He stated that his earnings were satisfactory and reasonable in comparison with the rest of the section ... but it was pointed out to him that the times that he was accepting though satisfactory to himself might not be acceptable to other operators who had to work these jobs after him ... he was now prepared to revise his outlook and demand more satisfactory times from his work in the future.

There had been a case on the centre lathes of a member accepting a bad time on a job when being advised against accepting. The convenor would have a word with him.

Regarding the acceptance of bad times by certain individuals who were conspicuous by their absence it was decided that such members would not be allowed to have a job timed without either the shop steward or the convenor in attendance.... It was up to all members of the section to expose jobs with bad times or individuals who accepted a bad time.... A member of the Capstan section who had been through a particularly rough period due to jobs with bad times had been brought before the Joint Shop Stewards' Committee and complimented on the manner in which he had stood up to members of the ratefixing department to secure his just rights.

Although factory B provided the strongest evidence of this sort of campaign against 'tight' job values, a few others provided indications of it. But it was not as common as the policy of controlling those who 'push it too far'. For instance, the convenor at F said that he did not do anything about those who accept tight values, despite his active policy against those at the other extreme.

There is evidence that these policies have a significant effect upon the dispersion of individual piecework earnings. At B where stewards restrained bargains at both ends the coefficient of variation of individual piecework earnings among skilled men was about 15 per cent. At factory A where stewards operated no constraint at all the coefficient of variation was about 25 per cent. Although this is not the only factor at work the data certainly support the contention that the stewards' policy is effective. The influence of the scatter of earnings upon their rate of drift was discussed in an earlier chapter.

SHOP STEWARDS' BEHAVIOUR TOWARDS C&P RULES

The control of individual piecework bargains is likely to have less effect upon the overall operation of piecework and the rate of non-negotiated drift than is the control of the rules whereby that bargaining proceeds. The role of stewards is of particular interest here because, as was demonstrated in the last chapter, C&P rules tend to drift so as to become more lenient to pieceworkers and so as to increase their individual bargaining power. Put simply, do stewards encourage or discourage C&P drift?

This is best discussed against the background of some illustrations. Once again the shop stewards' committee book of factory B is used. Since its records were never intended to be seen by anyone but the stewards themselves, and since they were recorded by several successive generations of officers over almost twenty years, there is no reason to suppose them a misleading source on steward motivations and action.

There is certainly evidence that stewards can be aggressive in ensuring that workers take full advantage of existing rules.[8]

> Shop stewards should see to it that operators were kept up to the mark in asking for estimated times on new jobs. It would be left to stewards to reprimand members for not obeying this procedure as they thought fit.

> There were operators in the shop who would not take advantage of the agreements between the Shop Stewards Committee and the Management. They were undoing much of the good work done in the shop and it was resolved that any person who failed in this respect should be brought before the Shop Stewards' Committee to give an explanation of his conduct.

There is also abundant evidence that stewards are vigilant in preventing management breaking existing C&P rules and in both advising on the content of those rules and taking action when they are broken.

> (The Fitting shop was on waiting time and the Works Manager approached the Convenor to say that he had alternative work for them and to ask) was he in order offering it? The Convenor stated that he was in order and had seen the shop stewards on fitting.

> There were some drilling jobs with times fixed at the development establishment. This would not hold water as it cut across all our agreements on piecework times and prices which were settled between ratefixer and operators. . . . An undertaking was given by the management that no interference of the character we had mentioned would take place.

[8] It should be noted that, in the quotations from the minute books that follow, the 'agreements' that are referred to are pure C&P rules. In most cases they were not written down and those that had been were recorded well after they became established.

A ratefixer had fixed the time for the job and then counted the pieces produced thus trying to place the operator in a position where he would have appeared to have swindled him over the job . . . (the Committee) should seek evidence on snooping if possible. (Subsequently, the Convenor) told the management that this trying to trap an operator would have serious repercussions in the shop. The Managing Director expressed his disapproval of the ratefixing section and had apologised to the Committee.

The Convenor had seen the Works Manager who agreed that the ratefixer had no right to ask the operator to increase feeds and speeds without consulting the setter or foreman.

In 1956 the Convenor raised the question of a C&P rule that new starters in the factory should only be timed after they had been there a fortnight. This was, he said, 'a common sense agreement and it is up to shop stewards to watch it. There had been instances where shop stewards had to insist that the rule be carried out.' In 1963 there is a record of a stoppage of work. 'A man had accepted a time for a job even though being new on the job. The ratefixers were accused of sharp practice.'

In this factory, then, it appears that a warning to top management is usually enough to prevent an encroachment upon a C&P rule but that in extreme circumstances a strike may be used. But, if it is clear that stewards are concerned that established rules should not be eroded by either workers or management, there is also evidence that they do not encourage their extension. Examples can be given of workers being brought into line for 'pushing things too far'.

The Chairman gave a word of warning regarding the booking of excessive hours pointing out that it was cutting the ground from under the negotiating committee's feet when they were engaged with the management on the question of times and wages. The Chairman stated that shop stewards should try to keep this under control on their sections as this was no doubt responsible for some of the jobs being sent out of the factory for operations.

(People were abusing amenities by leaving for the canteen early.) The convenor stated that there was a limit to this kind of conduct and that they should bring it to the attention of members. . . . The full responsibility would now rest with members in the shop who had only themselves to blame if disciplinary action were taken.

The Convenor referred to the tendency to increase feeds and speeds on the part of certain operators to try and make their time easier and then blaming this increase for any scrap resulting. There were adequate safeguards to see that times obtained were sufficient and no excuse was valid for altering feeds and speeds in this respect.

(A milling operator was having his times 'made up' by the foreman. The shop steward had told the foreman that this should not happen on a job that should be paying well on normal production) The Chairman suggested that in future when the operator approached the foremen to have his time made up he should be asked to supply a satisfactory explanation before any time should be granted.

The behaviour exhibited here is primarily protective. The stewards guard the established rules from anything that might alter them—whether or not such an alteration might appear superficially to be to their advantage. Similar (if less well documented) evidence could be given from other factories. Stewards do not appear to be concerned with provoking favourable precedents or with encouraging C&P drift. Such behaviour is very much the exception rather than the rule.

This behaviour towards C&P rules of job regulation is exactly complementary to the behaviour of stewards towards piecework wages described in the previous section. Stewards appear to be conservers rather than creators in informal shopfloor bargaining. They are the 'principal guardians of C&P'.[9] They come upon fresh C&P when it has already become established as legitimate in the minds of their members either because they are used to working that way or because the man whom they see as the boss connives

[9] A. Flanders, *Collective Bargaining: Prescription for Change*, London Faber, 1967, p. 69.

with them in it. It is when these ways of working are
threatened that the shop steward becomes involved in his
representative role and he has to defend C&P 'agreements'
that are as concrete as anything on paper in the minds of
his fellow workers.

The steward described here, it may be objected, is an
industrial eunuch. Does he never take the initiative? Does
he never act opportunistically? Are stewards to be relegated
to the position of nursemaids, fussing around to clear up
management messes and to keep their charges in order? In
order to answer these questions and also to account for the
variations in the behaviour of shop stewards from factory
to factory, it is necessary to look further at the forces moti-
vating stewards.

THE ROOTS OF SHOP STEWARD BEHAVIOUR

The power of shop stewards comes from the work groups
that they represent. This requires some definition of work
group. For industrial relations analysis the importance
of a work group lies in the bargaining power it possesses. It
can be seen as the smallest unit of a workforce which can
and does take effective collective action. It is a primary
group (that is, one linked by face-to-face relationships) in
which workers have a broadly common view on an issue
and are willing to act and capable of acting collectively to
further their interests in it.

The term 'work group' can be misleading in that it suggests that the group has a compactness and distinctiveness
that is often difficult to identify in practice. A worker may
act as member of one group on one issue and of another on
another. Work groups may wax and wane in both significance and size. They may form coalitions. But, however
they operate, they will find it difficult to use their collective
power effectively without a spokesman. If the spokesman is
to be an effective representative he will have to have continuity in the job and, like any other political representative,
besides following the wishes of those he represents, he will
at times have to take initiatives both in translating those

wishes into practical policies and in deciding how best they should be prosecuted. This representative—the shop steward—may represent one work group or many but it is likely that (unless his representation has been imposed from outside upon an apathetic part of the workforce) there will be considerable homogeneity of interest among his constituents.

The average shop steward is very much like the average trade union member.[10] The available data suggest that something between one in ten and one in twenty of all trade union members has been, is or will be a shop steward during the course of his or her working life.[11] Among piece-workers in the high Topsy factories in the current study the figure appeared to be nearer one in three or four. Thus the average piecework steward is unlikely to have unusual motivations. He is likely to pursue his representative duties in a way which, on the one hand, prevents him losing the sympathy of his constituents but, on the other, causes himself least inconvenience.

It is possible to discern four implicit principles of shop steward behaviour. The first two are the pursuit of unity and of equity among his constituents. These are closely interlinked. Sykes notes that in small printing chapels printers consider that 'unity among the members of the Chapel is vital to their interests, and that unity can be maintained only so long as members subordinate their individuality to the collective decision of the Chapel and maintain equality among themselves.'[12] He adds that 'the subordination of the individual to the authority of the asso-

[10] It should be noted that bargaining activity and the existence of workers' representatives is not restricted to trade union members alone. At factory E some powerful 'non-union representatives' sat beside conventional shop stewards on the works committee and, when management finally granted full recognition to the unions and the shop was closed to non-members, one of these earlier 'nonners' became a very effective factory convenor.

[11] This estimate is derived from the statistics given by the Government Social Survey, *op. cit.*

[12] A. J. M. Sykes, 'The Cohesion of a Trade Union Workshop Organisation', *Sociology*, 1967.

ciation is vital for its unity of action: equality before
authority is an essential condition for accepting subordination.'[13] Not only does equity encourage unity and hence
increase the workers' bargaining strength and the ease with
which the shop steward can call upon it; equity also
removes the jealousy and strife among workers that makes
everyday life unpleasant.

The third implicit principle of shop steward behaviour is
that of maintaining a good bargaining relationship with
management. Kuhn remarked that the shop steward provided the work group with 'a continuity and unity of
action'.[14] This continuity is of particular importance
in developing the link between workers and management.
The bargaining relationship that exists between a manager
and a shop steward (or between any other negotiating
opponents) consists in the confidence each can have
about his expectations of the other's behaviour. This
depends upon their mutual trust and respect and upon the
extent to which they share common assumptions and a
common language. A 'good' bargaining relationship may be
said to exist to the extent that these things help reduce the
uncertainty of the relationship.

The immediate advantage of a good bargaining relationship to a steward is, once again, a social one. The steward
and the managers he deals with have to operate with one
another on a continuing basis (and not only in the role of
bargainers) and a poor relationship would make life unbearable. The earlier chapter argued that this provided an
important reason for individual pieceworkers and ratefixers (or foremen) establishing common conceptions of
'fair' comparative reference groups which, in turn, was a
major factor in bringing stability to internal wage structures.

The more far-reaching advantage of the good bargaining

---

[13] *ibid*. It was noted earlier that the Royal Commission's survey
found that a principal reason for the unpopularity of piecework
among stewards was that it 'splits up the men'.

[14] J. W. Kuhn, *Bargaining in Grievance Settlement*, New York:
Columbia University Press, 1961, p. 80.

relationship is in speeding up the bargaining process and in making it less wasteful in terms of sanctions and misunderstandings. One convenor remarked to the writer that 'without trust you're like a conger eel on ice'. Walton and McKersie put this more academically when they observed that 'trust appears to be an unmixed asset in negotiations'.[15] For a negotiator, trust determines the degree of certainty he has that his opponent will 'observe the unwritten dictionary and ground rules' whenever the opponent might gain advantage in violating them. They emphasize the importance of trust in what they call 'intra-organizational' bargaining—that is, the job that a representative has to do to unify his supporters and to rally them to his point of view. For example, it may be important to a steward to pull the rug from under a militant group of his constituents by demonstrating to them that strike action is unproductive. He will be helped in this if he can be confident that management will not give way. Similarly, it may help a junior manager who is under pressure from his senior to 'get tough' with his workers if he knows that a token gesture in this direction will not lead to escalating counter-sanctions from the workforce. It should be added that, in the context of informal workshop bargaining, the ill-defined and fluid procedural positions that the protagonists often occupy make their bargaining relationships all the more important.

The pursuit of unity and equity among their constituents and of good bargaining relationships with management has immediate advantages, but they are also important as means to ends rather than as ends in themselves. They increase the power that the steward has to bargain with and also the economy with which he can use that power. The better a bargaining relationship the less likely it is that sanctions will need to be used. These three principles provide a basis for a steward (whether or not he is concerned with piecework) to make optimum use of the power at his disposal.

[15] R. E. Walton and R. B. McKersie, *A Behavioural Theory of Labor Negotiations*, New York: McGraw-Hill, 1965, p. 358.

To what end might he use them? The objectives of
shop steward action clearly vary with circumstances. The
one that at first sight might seem most obvious—that is, the
improvement of pay and conditions—is certainly not particularly evident in the case of piecework stewards in
situations of high non-negotiated drift. The simplest heading under which bargaining objectives might be grouped is
that of the reduction of uncertainty. This is, in any case, a
very broad heading. The deliberate exercise of power is
often aimed at making one's world a more predictable place
to live in. But in the context of piecework it is particularly
important. The second reason given by stewards for dislik-
ing piecework in the Royal Commission's survey was that it
made earnings fluctuate. The stabilization of earnings is a
major steward activity. The extracts from the minute books
revealed both steward concern about future work prospects
and the action that was taken to work more cautiously
when redundancies were feared. A similar concern with uncertainty reduction is evident in efforts to maintain established differentials between workers and also in the importance attached to preserving a good bargaining relationship.
On empirical evidence it seems fair to conclude that a
fourth principle of shop steward behaviour (certainly in the
case of piecework stewards) is the reduction of uncertainty
in his constituents' relationships with management.

The roots of shop steward behaviour, then, are these
linked preoccupations with unity, equity, the preservation
of the bargaining relationship, and the reduction of uncertainty. These four principles are the essence of 'shop-
stewardliness'. Individual stewards will conform to these
principles to a greater or lesser extent, but the principles will
tend to show through in the regular patterns of behaviour
of groups of stewards. How far they show through, and how
successfully the principles are pursued, will depend upon the
nature of the shop stewards' organization.

THE INTEGRATION OF THE SHOP STEWARD BODY

It is necessary first to say something about the impact

upon factory shop steward organizations of outside factors. The most obvious of these is that of the national trade unions. At all the ten plants studied there were at least three unions covering pieceworkers and other unions organized some of the indirect workers. All the factories were heavily unionized and almost all had one hundred per cent unionization. None had any inter-union disputes of importance. The situation was, in fact, just as Turner, Clack and Roberts described in their account of 'parallel-unionism'. 'What union a man is actually a member of has, for many operatives at least, largely become irrelevant so long as he is a subscriber'.[16] Some factories had joint shop steward committees which had constitutional provisions to share the main committee offices among the major unions present, but for others this had died out. The full-time union officials were generally on excellent terms with the senior stewards and appeared to be quite happy to leave them to look after themselves, going into the factories only occasionally to sort out intractable deadlocks and to attend formal works conferences when disputes were put into the EEF/CSEU disputes procedure. If multi-unionism hindered shop-floor union organization, there was no evidence of it. Stewards represented everyone within their geographical constituency irrespective of union label and sometimes even factory convenors came from minority unions.

In their study of the car industry, Turner, Clack and Roberts noted that 'in general the stewards' organization is under pressures that compel it towards certain responsible patterns of institutional behaviour—"responsible" at least in the sense that its leaders are obliged to balance a variety of group interests against the particular sectional claims with which they are confronted, and to bear in mind the long-term desirability of maintaining good negotiating relations with management'.[17] This is close to saying that stewards' organizations are under pressures to follow the first three principles discussed in the previous section—the

[16] Turner, Clack and Roberts, *op. cit.*, p. 222.
[17] *ibid.*, p. 222.

principles of unity, of equity and of good bargaining relationships. It is not surprising that the principles that permit
the individual steward to make most efficient use of the
power at his disposal are also effective for steward committees. For the job of the committee is that of the individual
steward writ large with the added problem that there will
be more divergent interests within a factory's workforce
than within a steward's constituency. To a large extent
stewards' constituencies are self-selecting to bring uniformity of interests within each. By contrast, the heterogeneity
of interests within a whole factory is something that a
stewards' committee has to live with.

Through the pursuit of the four principles of 'shop-
stewardliness', a stewards' committee can not only make
optimum use of the workforce's bargaining power, it can
also help its member stewards in their own pursuit of the
principles. Consequently, it is not surprising that across much
of post-war British industry, shop stewards bodies have
emerged and developed in very similar ways despite there
having been little cross-fertilization between them and despite the lack of guidance from their national unions.

In order to illustrate how a shop steward body pursues
these principles it is useful to describe some operational
indicators. The extent to which unity is achieved is relatively
easy to identify. Does the whole factory take collective action
when need be or do some sections (for instance the tool-
makers) remain aloof? Does the stewards' committee
attempt to coordinate wage claims for time-workers, or do
the different groups of labourers, setters, material handlers
and so on have to submit their own claims without any
common strategy? Does the committee have the power—
either by commanding effective social sanctions or by
threatening to abandon those concerned—to discipline sections of the workforce which endanger the bargaining
relationship by 'pushing things too far'?

Assessing the effectiveness with which equity is pursued
is made more difficult by the fact that there are usually
established inequities such as, for instance, between crafts-

men and mates, which the shop stewards may not question. But the scatter of individual earnings within a skill-grade will be a useful indicator. So also will be stewards' policy on overtime allocation and on the prevention of piece-workers accepting 'tight' piecework values. Some steward bodies have active policies to 'stop the poor old labourer falling behind' and these show through clearly when stewards participate in job evaluation schemes.

The nature of the bargaining relationship with management is likely to be reflected in the procedural position given to stewards. It will also show in the use of collective sanctions by workers and in the extent to which jobs are regulated unilaterally by workers as against jointly with management. *A priori* one would expect a good bargaining relationship to be accompanied by a sparing use of sanctions and a large measure of joint regulation.

The success with which the steward body is able to insulate workers from uncertainties is to be gauged by, among other things, the stability of individual earnings and the guarantees that have been negotiated against lay-offs. It will also be reflected in the extent of worker regulation—unilateral or joint—over work.

The illustrations will be sufficient to demonstrate that the shop steward body that is capable of pursuing the principles of 'shop-stewardliness' with success is a sophisticated political organisation. Such a body might be termed 'integrated' in that it is able to accommodate the diverse and potentially conflicting interests of different sections of the workforce under a single policy-making and negotiating executive. Through a hierarchy of elected representatives it is capable of using the maximum bargaining strength of the labour force at the same time as protecting minority interests among workers.

A tightly integrated shop steward committee is likely to be jealous of its centralized authority and to resent any attempts to by-pass it. This is illustrated by another quotation from factory B's steward committee minute book:

The Convenor expressed his disgust of the fact that during this case (the suspension of some men for excessive scrap) one of the men involved contacted the management to restate his case, without first informing the Convenor of his intention. This type of action must not be permitted to happen again; by doing this the man has jeopardised the position of the Shop Stewards' Committee for which he has been reprimanded.

Such a committee is also likely to develop for itself a solid base in written documents. Its own standing orders are likely to be important in times of disagreement between stewards. A newsheet may keep workers in touch with negotiations. Minutes of its own meetings and of meetings with management will help resolve disagreements and strengthen the committee's bargaining position with management. The Fleet Street printing chapels often place great reliance upon their minute books as guides for future action and sources of precedent. In an industry like engineering where the legitimacy of custom and precedent is so strong, a stewards' committee can often put itself in a stronger position than management by maintaining better archives. The case of the 'grubby piece of paper' in the previous chapter illustrates this.

Despite the fact that there are pressures on a shop steward body to become integrated in order to make most efficient use of its power, in practice not all of them move in this direction. Shop steward committees vary very much in their degree of integration. Nor does this appear to depend upon the willingness of the workforce to bargain over issues. This can be illustrated by a contrast between factories A and B.

In superficial terms A and B are very similar. They are about the same size and age; they have very similar technologies; they are within a few miles of each other; they have the same ownership characteristics; their labour forces have about the same skill, age and length of service distribution; and they have the same trade unions representing the workers. There appears to be nothing to choose between them in terms of bargaining propensity. In both, piece-workers bargained job values individually and overtime bans and stoppages were used in both.

In terms of the integration of the shop steward body, however, they differed considerably. The stewards at A had little impact upon individual bargains and the dominant pieceworking stewards made no attempt to coordinate or assist the claims of indirect workers. The committee kept no minutes, had no standing orders and kept few records. Stoppages were more frequent than at B and were generally more partial. Some groups—notably electricians and tool-makers—periodically opted out of the committee altogether. Mistrust of management by the senior stewards was considerable. The contrast that B presented on these points was complete. The extracts from the committee minutes that were given earlier testify to the constitutionality and powers of the stewards. The apparent effect of their piece-work policy upon the scatter of individual earnings has already been commented on. The committee had relatively little trouble with deviant sections and it was accorded a high procedural status by management.

These two factories can also be used to illustrate two further points about the nature of shop stewards' organisations of different degrees of integration. The question raised is how much these different organizational characteristics influence the sort of people who become stewards and the way in which they act. The evidence that is available on this is very slender but is of interest both as an indicator of the answer and as an illustration of the use of quantitative tests in this sort of study.

The first scrap of evidence is the average length of time that shop stewards spend in office. *A priori* one would expect that a more constitutional system would ease the pressures on individual stewards or, failing that, provide them with more support in their bargaining. Both this and greater electoral satisfaction would be expected to keep stewards in office longer. The Royal Commission survey found that stewards interviewed from the T&GWU had been in office an average of 6 years and those from the AEU an average of 5 years. A non-engineering factory in Coventry (studied by the writer) with a predominantly timeworking labour force showed an average length of steward service of 6 years with 50 per cent of them having been in office for over 4 years. By contrast—and in interesting confirmation of the dissatisfactions raised by piecework —the factories with pieceworking show much shorter periods in office with an average of 2 years at A, E and C (where only 20 per cent had more than 4 years service). By contrast at B the average length of time that had been spent in office was 4 years and 55 per cent of stewards had held office for more than 4 years. In brief, this is positive support of the hypothesis that an integrated steward body has greater stability of membership. There is also the interesting corollary that the high turnover of a weak steward committee will reduce its continuity and hence also its bargaining relationship and its strength and constitutionality still more.

The second straw in the wind is still more flimsy. It is the personal earnings of piecework stewards. At B the individual earnings records were studied for two periods of several months several years apart. It was found that the average earnings of stewards were not significantly different (in the statistical sense) from the averages of the sections on which they worked. At A, however, three of the four dominant stewards earned consistently (over several years) at least 40 per cent above their section averages. Two were always top of their sections and the third was always in the top three. The fourth was an elderly man whose earnings were average. These high earnings were generally known to management and they did not ascribe them to exceptional effort or skill. The stewards appeared, in the words of Tom Lehrer, to be 'doing well by doing good'. This could be interpreted various ways. It may be that the senior steward's job in an unintegrated organization is so unrewarding in the normal way that the only people who are willing to take it on are those who see it (with a little help from indulgent junior management) as a way to extra cash. Weak though it is, this evidence suggests that a poorly integrated shop steward body attracts fairly opportunistic senior stewards.

Why it is that some steward bodies should become integrated while others remain fragmented will be returned to later. First we must look at the implications of this hypothesis of shop steward organization for the development of C&P rules.

WORKFORCE CHARACTERISTICS AND THE GROWTH OF C&P

It is useful to see workshop bargaining as taking place within three crude dimensions (perhaps more accurately termed 'vectors'). The first is the 'bargaining awareness' of the workforce. The second is its power over management. The third is the degree of integration of the shop steward body.

What, for want of a better term, has been called 'bargaining awareness' is the most difficult of these to analyse. A workforce may be said to have a bargaining awareness on some aspect of work when it recognizes that conflicts of interest might arise on it and that it is potentially negotiable. It is a phenomenon of relatively full employment when workers' aspirations are raised and when they can have confidence in their possession of bargaining power. But this is not a sufficient explanation. People in very similar employment situations show very different degrees of willingness to challenge their managements. Even among those who do so freely, the issues upon which the challenge is made vary considerably.

It appears that employees can gain bargaining awareness on an issue from a number of causes. It may be that management has manifestly failed to protect their interests—for instance by permitting working conditions to become unbearable, or by letting the pay of one section fall far below that of its neighbour because of a technical oversight. It may be that a group of workers has always felt inhibited from using its bargaining power by a feeling of social or vocational obligation but that, when they see a comparable group using it with consequences that are rewarding and not catastrophic, they revise their view. It may be that communications improvements cause workers to widen their comparative reference groups to include other workers who do bargain effectively on matters. However it comes about, once workers have come to question the right and/or ability of management to protect their interests unilaterally, and once they appreciate their own capability of influencing management on the issue concerned, they are unlikely to take it on trust again. The process is usually irreversible.

This bargaining awareness can vary both in intensity and in the issues it covers—pay, working conditions, mobility, level of effort and so on—and its strength can vary within a workplace. Although a workforce that has bargaining awareness on one issue is the more likely to gain it on another, it need not do so if it is given no cause for disquiet. Thus bargaining awareness usually does not come to a workforce as enlightenment came to Saul. It usually comes gradually if it comes at all. Nor is it fruitful to ask whether it is 'good' or 'bad'; it is an empirical condition of the workers concerned. But it is the basis upon which workshop bargaining rests.

The second vector influencing workshop bargaining is that of the power of the workforce. Bargaining power is the capability of influencing the actions of management in a deliberate and predictable way through the collective actions of workers. As Dunlop has shown[18] it depends upon many factors over which the workforce has no control. The two most important of these are the production technology and the product market. It is, for instance, easier to disrupt a production process that has long integrated flow lines than one that has brief and unrelated operations. Similarly it is easier to distress management where the product market is highly competitive and the product perishable than where the market is secure and the product easily stock-piled.

The third vector is the degree of integration of the shop

[18] J. T. Dunlop, *Industrial Relations Systems*, New York: Holt, 1958.

steward body. Although these three vectors are best seen as distinct from one another, they influence each other strongly. The development of bargaining awareness and the exercise of power, for instance, reinforce each other. Again, a shop steward organization is unlikely to achieve a substantial degree of integration unless the workforce has a high degree of bargaining awareness. A workforce does not necessarily have equivalent strength in all these respects, however. Factory A, as has been discussed, was strong on awareness but weak on integration. Factory K, on the other hand, was fairly strong on power and integration but weak in awareness.

The purpose of this simple framework is to provide a setting for understanding the circumstances in which C&P will flourish and drift. Bargaining awareness is necessary before individual workers and work groups will appreciate the significance of the chance errors of management which constitute precedents. It is necessary if they are to feel a sense of grievance when an established custom is revoked by management. Bargaining power is necessary if they are to defend established customs and precedents from management efforts to revoke them. The more a workforce has of these qualities the more likely it is, other things being equal, that C&P will emerge and drift. But what of the integration of the shop steward body? How does this influence the development of C&P rules?

Taking the hypothesis of shop steward organization that has been developed, together with the illustrations from the committee minute book, it is possible to answer this with some confidence. The growing integration of the shop steward body increases its ability to pursue the implicit principles of unity, equity, a good bargaining relationship and the reduction of uncertainty. It increases the tendency of the stewards to adopt established C&P and to turn it into 'agreements' which are a firm basis for dealing with management. Deviants among workers (whether they fall below or push above the norm concerned) will be forced into line by informal sanctions. Precedents that are favourable to workers are likely to be ironed out by a committee which sees greater advantage in preserving its bargaining relationship with management by protecting established rules. In short, in matters of C&P as in matters of wages, an integrated shop steward body is a force for stability. It is also a force restricting the development of C&P drift.

There is an obvious paradox here. Despite the fact that C&P tends to drift in a way that makes rules more generous to individual workers, it is being argued that, the more integrated a shop steward body becomes, the more it will try to prevent this drift. Because C&P drifts despite rather than because of shop stewards, an increase in their control will reduce the non-negotiated drift in both C&P and wages. Is the conclusion of the argument to be that growing political sophistication makes shop stewards resemble more than ever management-oriented nursemaids?

In order to answer this it is necessary to recall some of the observations of the previous chapter on the way in which C&P develops. It was noted that, in drifting, C&P tends to shift a wide range of matters into unilateral worker control because, by so doing, it reduced the uncertainty of the individual pieceworker's earnings and increased his bargaining power. Yet some of these wider matters implied much farther reaching strategies. They included, in the examples given, worker control of the feeds and speeds of operation and of the mobility of labour between jobs. There was no evidence that these broader strategies had ever been formulated by workers. Indeed, all the evidence pointed against it. The central characteristic of C&P growth is the *lack of intention* behind it. Put another way, it is of no avail to look at the end result of a process of C&P drift and to ask the question 'why?' and expect an answer in terms of the motives of individuals or of groups. The state of C&P rules after such a process of drift will be the consequence of the accretion of a host of uncoordinated actions. The principal actors will have had no conception of what the aggregate of their diverse actions will look like and no deliberate intention of bringing it about.

It could still be argued that, although stewards have little or no control over C&P drift, they may be aware that it tends to operate to increase the area of unilateral worker control and to make the rules of job regulation more lenient to workers. And, because of this, stewards might be expected to encourage it; they may not be able to control the wind but they know that it can only bring them good.

But this presupposes that it is necessarily better from the shop stewards' point of view to have more indulgent rules and a greater span of unilateral control. More specifically, one can question whether it is desirable to have such rules and such control when they have been achieved in a higgledy-piggledy way and when they sap the collective power of the workforce. Certainly shop stewards appear to question this.[19] One steward commented very critically on a C&P rule whereby workers were paid average earnings when a job value was in dispute; he felt that such a generous rate of payment encouraged the more unscrupulous pieceworkers to waste stewards' time by stringing out negotiations and that it gave rise to anomalies in earnings. A similar instance was provided in the quotation from the steward who was opposed to the inequities of the 'jungle' of a piecework system with which he worked where a man's earnings were determined by whether he was working on a new model or an old one.

From the steward's point of view, piecework systems in an advanced stage of C&P drift are usually grotesque monuments to the inefficient use of bargaining power. They breed and nurture the inequities, the disunities, the uncertainties and the poor bargaining relationships which are anathema to the steward's implicit principles. One convenor

[19] There is, of course, a further school of thought on this issue. This would see the process of 'integration' of shop stewards described here as one in which stewards divorce themselves from the aspirations of the rank and file and thus, according to the same school, follow in the footsteps of most full-time trade union officers in compromising with capitalism. Whether or not this is based upon a fair view of worker aspirations is, in the absence of significant evidence, a matter of personal judgement. The theory of collective action it implies seems as forlorn as it is romantic.

who had been a negotiator many years earlier when his factory's piecework system had been installed described his feelings graphically: 'We created this baby . . . but now it is thinking for itself. It is operating in a way we never intended. The child has become a monster.'

THE ROLE OF SHOP STEWARDS IN STRIKES

At this stage of the argument it may be more clear why stewards tend to act so as to reduce C&P drift, but, to many observers, the sort of role described so far may seem unconvincingly placid. The obvious place to turn for more clues is the most notorious and unplacid area of industrial relations: what role do stewards play in strikes?

Strikes are appallingly difficult subjects of study. There are two reasons for doubting whether any brief discussion of them can be rewarding. The first was well discussed by the social anthropologist Malinowski who found it most profitable to make a study 'of the law obeyed and not the law broken; of the permanent currents and tides in . . . social life and not its adventitious storms'.[20] The second reason is simply that a great diversity of human behaviour tends to be bundled under the general term 'strike' and this carries the misleading implication that different strikes have more than the superficial in common. With this qualification, however, and in the knowledge that many people do consider strikes to be very important in themselves, do workshop strikes happen because of, or in spite of, shop steward activity?

Turner, Clack and Roberts concluded that the stewards in their study of the motor industry do not 'appear as stimulating disputes. Rather, they are attempting to control a number of pressures to which they are subject, including those from management and outside union officials, but especially including pressures from particular groups and sections of workpeople themselves. Which is not to say that leading stewards (or, for that matter, local union officers)

[20] B. Malinowski, *Crime and Custom in Savage Society*, London: Routledge and Kegan Paul, 1926, p. 73.

Goo forward
3 pp!

piecework systems in the 1950s and little or no documentation of agreements has remained from that time.

It soon became apparent why there was no documentation of this sort. For at least seven of the ten factories studied, the rules that actually prevailed had little or no resemblance to those that had originally been laid down by management or by formal agreement. The piecework systems operated according to transactional rules certainly, and these rules were generally known and recognized as legitimate by both the workers and the managers involved. But they had no formal origin in an explicit negotiation between representatives of the two sides.

In a minority of factories there were, it is true, some written agreements. They covered such matters as the procedure for ratefixing and the levels of pay when machines broke down, and they were often signed by representatives of management and by shop stewards and were treated as formal agreements. On further inspection, however, it became evident that these documents represented no more than 'snapshots' of the current state of the transactional rules already in being when they were signed. With a very few exceptions (which will receive attention in the next chapter) the apparent formality of these rules was misleading because they had never come into being through explicit negotiations. Indeed, in some cases the apparent formal workshop agreements of the past had become submerged and negated by the subsequent development of unwritten, informal transactional rules.

On the evidence of the case studies it appears that all or most of the important transactional rules regulating the conduct of piecework, especially in factories with high Topsy factors, have informal origins. This informality is not just a consequence of being outside national negotiations which was the principal use made of the term by the Donovan Commission. They are informal in that they are non-negotiated in the same sense as in the earlier discussion of wage drift. They do not arise from a process of explicit negotiation in which the recognized representatives of workers and

D

management appreciate that they are establishing a transactional rule.

The name given to these rules in Midlands engineering (and elsewhere) is 'custom and practice' (C&P) and it will be used generically. The rest of this chapter is concerned with C&P rules because they appear to be the type of transactional rule that is most important to the conduct of piecework in factories with powerful workforces. Since these rules have received virtually no attention from academic analysis in the past, it will be necessary to present a considerable amount of empirical data to support the assertions made about them.

THE CONTENT AND DIVERSITY OF C&P RULES OF PIECEWORK

The purpose of this section is to demonstrate the variation of C&P rules between factories and to show how this influences the relative power of the bargainers. Four different areas of the piecework bargain will be selected for study. Reference will be made to the relevant clauses in the national engineering agreements as a sort of datum line although, as Chapter One noted, these have never been universally applied.

a) THE PRINCIPAL AGENTS INVOLVED IN THE BARGAIN

The national agreement says that piecework job values 'shall be fixed by mutual arrangement between the employer and the worker who is to perform the work. . . .' In practice one can find deviations from this in two different directions. In one factory, where management control was undisputed, the general pattern was for the work study engineer to select a competent operator whom he then timed working at the job. Having calculated the allowed time for it he handed it over to the foreman concerned. The foreman then offered it to the worker for whom the job was initially intended but, if that worker refused to accept the value, the foreman was then free to offer it about among the other workers on the section. One foreman observed that 'we usually find someone who will accept it in the end'. A shop steward in the same factory commented resignedly that 'some people are soft enough to accept anything'. At another factory it was the rule that piecework values were agreed between ratefixers and company chargehands without any reference to workers or their representatives. When challenged by trade unions this rule was upheld by the National Arbitration Tribunal on the grounds that it was an established practice.

The more normal procedure in the factories studied was broadly according to the national agreement: the ratefixer would estimate the value for the job after watching the man who was to work with it in future and would then negotiate the value with the same man. But sometimes there were restrictions on this, such as the rule that no pieceworker could be given a work study until he had been in the factory for six months. A more extreme deviation was the procedure whereby the shop steward was able to select the operator for the ratefixer to study whether or not that man was subsequently to work on the job in question. Stewards in these cases made no secret of the fact that they usually chose the worker whom they considered to be the most adept at confusing the ratefixer.

In the actual bargain that takes place after the study, it is not uncommon to find that someone other than the operator concerned concludes the agreement for him. While this was usually his own shop steward, cases are on record where it is done by a departmental committee of shop stewards. How this intervention by shop stewards will influence the outcome of the bargain is to be discussed in the next chapter. The varying role of management representatives in the bargain and the effect of their control systems upon this will also be left until later. For the moment it is sufficient to note that the less the control that C&P gives management over the worker who is involved in the study and bargain, the less control it will have over the earnings that result.

b) THE FREEDOM OF WORK STUDY

It has already been emphasized how important it is to management's control of earnings for ratefixers and work study engineers to be able to calculate accurate 'floor-to-floor times'. How far this can be achieved depends upon the precision with which timing and effort rating can be carried out. A major restriction on this can be the C&P rules.

The best known instance of rules that restrict work study is a ban on the use of stop watches. This is often coupled with a ban on overt effort rating and on the timing of separate 'elements'. More moderate rules permit the use of wrist watches—some explicitly permitting the use of sweep second hands on them. These rules are not simply the result of managements' being too backward in introducing refined work study techniques; in one factory the workforce was able to bring an end to the use of stop watches in some departments on the basis of the argument that they were not permitted elsewhere in the works. Other types of rules can have a similar effect in inhibiting effective time measurement during work study. For instance, one rule permitted work study engineers to time only one cycle of work when they were studying a job—although, without watches, they were permitted to observe as many cycles as they wished.

Moving away from the question of timing work, the rules helping or hindering effective work study show considerable variety. On the side of helping, some establishments have rules that require the operator to test the job value that the work study engineer first offers. In one place, for instance, operators could not refuse a proposed piecework job value (and hence not start to bargain over it) until they had worked at it for at least one hour. The work study engineers concerned said that this was usually effective in quelling initial complaints and in getting the proposed value accepted.

Rules that hinder work study are instanced by those that inhibit the work study engineer's control over the speed at which machines are run while they are observing the job. Examples of these will be discussed at some length later in this chapter. Another topic where rules may be important is that of demonstrations by management that a job value is fair. The national agreement which relates to the general workers' unions[4] states that '... it is desirable where exception is taken to a price, bonus or basis time proposed by the management that the latter should by demonstration justify the proposal made whenever practicable or feasible.' It appears to be the case however that, even where only the general unions are involved, management demonstrations are usually banned by C&P.

c) THE CIRCUMSTANCES IN WHICH NEW JOB VALUES MAY BE NEGOTIATED

When a new job appears in a factory there is usually little question but that a value should be negotiated for it. Much more contentious are the cases that occur when an established job is altered in some way, or when the passage of time makes its value become excessively 'tight'. Rules that regulate this large area of uncertainty are important because they have a marked effect upon the frequency with which piecework values can be renegotiated. The greater this frequency, the greater is likely to be the rate of non-negotiated wage drift that results.

The national agreements lay down certain principles for reobservation:

'No piecework prices, bonus or basis times once established may be altered except for the following reasons:-

1. A mistake in the calculation on either side, or
2. The material, means or method of production or the quantities are changed, or
3. A mutual arrangement has been come to between the employer and the worker in the same way as a new price is arranged.'[5]

[4] CSEU Handbook of Agreements in the Engineering Industry.
[5] Agreement between the CSEU and EEF, 1931.

It requires no expertise to appreciate how these clauses are open to ambiguous and tendentious interpretation. In particular, number (2) is very differently interpreted in different establishments. In some places renegotiation cannot take place without the justification of a complete change in the product while in others the periodic 'facelift' of a model will be taken as the opportunity to renegotiate all piecework values connected with it even though the number of technical changes that have been made is very small. Unless piecework values are given for small 'elements' of a job it is common for minor changes on a long job to require the rate-fixers to renegotiate the value for the entire job.

In all but the most docile factories it is normal for provision (1) to be over-ruled by C&P that forbids the rectification of mistakes by management in fixing piecework values if those mistakes are favourable to workers. In some cases the writer has met particularly glaring and anomalous consequences of work study error that have been referred to specifically as 'irreversible because they're C&P'.

The most common situation in which there is a demand for reobservation arises when operators feel that their earnings are inadequate because their piecework values were fixed some time in the past when prevailing wages were considerably lower. In some establishments there is no way of rectifying this. Workers apparently come to accept that they must take 'the rough with the smooth'. In others rules exist to permit men to appeal for the reobservation of such jobs. One form of rule sets the age of the piecework value as the criterion; for instance, one such rule said that any job whose value was fixed more than four years ago was entitled to be revalued. Another form of rule relates the criterion to the earnings that the job yields. Under this a man may, for instance, appeal for a reobservation if his earnings are 'unreasonably low within his section'.

One provision of the national agreements is that 'When the material, means or method of production is changed and the employer desires a modification in price or basis time, the modification shall in no case be such as to effect a reduction in the earnings of the workers concerned.'[6] In some cases this is effectively ignored and such a change can then bring an uncompensated loss of earnings to the worker concerned. Other factories have rules that uphold this provision and require that the altered job should be restudied if the worker is likely to suffer financially. In some cases a provision is made for a 'learning period' in which pieceworkers can become accustomed to the changed job before appeal for a reobservation can be made.

The ambiguities of this provision of the agreement blossom into confusion when the job that a man is working on changes completely. In fact most factories have rough but adequate rules which pin down the point at which a change in 'material, means or methods' is so extreme that it constitutes a new job. For some the distinction is irrelevant because C&P rules require that the pieceworker's earnings should not drop in any circumstances whether the job alters slightly or fundamentally. The case of men being moved away from their usual machine raises similar issues. In some factories such a move must not be accompanied by a loss in earnings in any circumstances. In others it must not be accompanied by a loss in earnings only if it is done as a favour to management when work is still available at the pieceworker's normal machine. In others again, no rules require management to make any sort of compensation at all for moving pieceworkers about.

Given this variety of rules it might be expected that the whole question of the transferability of piecework values between workers would, in places, be called into doubt. It is, after all, an unusual principle that once an individual has agreed a piecework value for himself that value is binding upon anyone who subsequently performs the job. Unusual or not, this principle is adhered to with remarkable consistency in almost all circumstances. Where pieceworkers try to dodge it they usually argue that their predecessor on the job agreed the value long ago and that it

[6] Agreement between the NFGW and EEF, 1920.

is technically due for reappraisal on that count. In one situation the case studies showed interesting examples of diversions from this principle. That was the situation in which a new job was introduced for both day and night shifts at the same time. In this circumstance two factories had developed C&P procedures whereby the value accepted by a man on one shift could be queried by his counterpart on the other shift and referred back to him for renegotiation.

d) THE LEVEL OF PAY WHEN PIECEWORK VALUES ARE IN DISPUTE

Apart from those factories where, as has been described, the labour force is so passive that management can, in effect, impose piecework values, the outcome of the piecework bargain depends in part upon the relative cost of disagreement to the two parties. From the management's point of view, a failure to reach agreement on a piecework negotiation threatens loss of production. From the worker's point of view, it threatens loss of pay.

This requires elaboration. At one extreme there is a practice referred to by one author[7] as '. . . the old Coventry tradition of putting the job on the floor, which means that the operator refuses to do the job until he gets satisfaction.' This sort of action merges into overt collective sanctions such as sectional stoppages and overtime bans which will be discussed later. Probably more commonly the pieceworker works at the new job even though it has no piecework value but he works at well below his normal piecework effort. He does this partly because he has little incentive to work harder as he is probably being paid a time-rate. But, in addition, he knows that his low level of output puts pressure upon management to concede. The longer he can spin work out, the more favourable the final outcome is likely to be to him.

Consequently it becomes important to consider the cost to him of not getting a piecework value agreed for his job. The

[7] P. Higgs, 'The Convenor' in R. Fraser (ed) *Work*, London: Pelican, 1969, p. 113.

national agreements lay down one basis for payment in these circumstances:

> Pending an arrangement being come to regarding a piecework price, bonus or basis time, the worker shall proceed with the job in accordance with the piecework price, bonus or basis time allowed by the management.[8]

In other words, until agreement has been reached, the operator continues to work piecework on management's terms. At none of the factories studied was this rule followed. One refinement of it that was intended to be effective at one factory was that workers should work at the rate proposed by management until agreement was reached and then that they should be paid retrospectively the difference between the final value and the proposed value for all the work they had done meanwhile. But even this apparently rational device was falling into disuse as foremen were increasingly succumbing to pressure from workers to pay them (by devious methods) their average earnings until agreement was reached. A moment's reflection reveals the source of the reluctance of workers to follow this ostensibly fair procedure. It weakens their bargaining strength by removing the pressures on management to improve upon the value initially proposed.

Much more common when there is a failure to agree over a piecework value is for the worker to be paid a fixed time-rate while still working at the new job. The time-rate that is paid varies between factories. The lowest that the case studies showed amounted to 75 per cent of average piecework earnings. At different factories it ranged up through 80 and 90 per cent to full average earnings. The implication of this variation is clear; the consequence to the worker of failing to agree a piecework value can, at one extreme, mean a loss of one quarter of earnings until agreement is reached and, at the other, no loss at all. In the latter position the pieceworker is unlikely to reach agreement with the ratefixer until there is no doubt in his mind that the

[8] CSEU, *op. cit.*

agreed job value will yield earnings at least as good as his present average earnings. In this situation management is almost incapable of resisting new values that significantly increase piecework earnings.

The four areas of rules governing the piecework bargain that have been described by no means exhaust the points at which C&P rules regulate the power relationship between the two parties. But they do illustrate how this regulation occurs and how great a variation in rules there can be from factory to factory. It will help at this stage to say a little more about the nature of C&P rules.

THE LOCALIZATION AND STABILITY OF C&P

The wide variation in C&P rules between different factories has already been discussed at some length. An interesting characteristic of C&P is that considerable variation can also occur within individual establishments. Some of this can be easily accounted for in terms of technical features. For instance, if one department is more prone to interruptions in work than its neighbours, then it is likely to develop special rules to cope with this. An example comes from one section of a factory where men had to change from machine to machine much more than in the rest of the plant. Because earnings suffered as a result of this, a C&P rule was developed whereby, if they were moved more than three times in one shift, they would be guaranteed their average earnings.

Other variations are not so easily accounted for. In one factory the management introduced a new cost-control system and, with it, a rule that operators should 'clock on and off' when they started and completed jobs. One department ignored this (thereby continuing to benefit from the 'fiddling' of setting and waiting times) and its foreman failed to press for compliance. He subsequently said that 'it didn't matter all that much that they didn't use the time-clock'. Within a few weeks the continuance of the old practice had completely over-ruled the new system in that department and management was forced to attempt to 'buy out' the

C&P rule. It is not only weak supervision that can give rise to this situation. Another instance comes from a factory where the machine shop was exceptionally aggressive and united compared with the other shops. Apparently as a result of this several rules were unique to the machine shop within the factory. It had more generous compensation for workers when they failed to reach agreement on piecework values. It refused to permit the use of stop watches by work study engineers even though they used them without question elsewhere in the factory. It also differed in having a C&P rule giving full average payment as compensation to pieceworkers when they were moved between machines.

It would be misleading to conclude that anomalous C&P rules arise and continue solely because of variations in worker attitudes and strength or in the fallibility of foremen. One wholly irrational anomaly was found in a factory where management had quite exceptionally close control over the piecework system and over a docile and largely female workforce. The department concerned was very similar to others in the factory but it was the rule to add 20 per cent on to every piecework value fixed in it. It turned out that this dated back to a time 15 years earlier when development work had caused work to be interrupted and broken into short batches. The C&P rule had continued unchanged although its justification had long since vanished. Interestingly, those immediately concerned among both management and workers were largely unaware of the origin of the anomaly; they were quite happy to accept it as a fact of life.

This last instance suggests that C&P rules can have great stability and yet not serve as precedents even when they are conspicuous. This is certainly not always the case. In many instances they can spread rapidly. For instance, the banning of stop watches may be a localized C&P rule in some factories and can persist as such for years. But in one factory already referred to the convenor of stewards said that when he had 'discovered' that stop watches were being used in some departments while they were banned in others he

quickly made the ban universal. Another common example
is that of a concession being made on payment for waiting
time by an indulgent foreman in one section which, when
discovered by workers elsewhere, spreads rapidly to neighbouring sections and beyond.

The similarities between the behaviour of C&P rules
described here and of wage differentials described at the end
of the previous chapter need no emphasis. Clearly similar
factors are at work in the formation and insulation of reference groups. Generally, however, it appears that integrated
shop steward bodies are more willing to 'universalize' a C&P
rule that has become established in one part of their plant
than they are to do the same with a favourable wage
differential. One can only speculate that spreading a C&P
rule puts less strain on their bargaining relationship with
management than spreading a favourable wage differential.
Perhaps also workers are more sensitive to 'C&P differentials' than they are to established wage differentials.

The Development of Custom and Practice Rules

The emphasis which has been placed upon the importance of
C&P rules for the balance of power in the piecework bargain
makes it necessary to explore the way in which C&P
emerges and develops. An example will provide a basis for
discussion.

THE 'AVERAGE BONUS' EXAMPLE

The factory in question had a piecework system based upon
fairly rudimentary ratefixing. The earlier section of this
chapter has mentioned the importance to the piecework
bargain of the level of payment when a pieceworker
has failed to agree on a piecework value for his job with the
ratefixer. In this case the payment used to be a time-rate of
approximately 80 per cent of earnings although foremen had
some discretionary powers to pay extra in special circumstances.

In their efforts to gain the cooperation of the men, foremen used this discretion with increasing liberality until in 1960 a senior manager, unwittingly, put verbal approval upon the payment of 'average bonus' for most circumstances. He did this in settlement of a dispute unaware of the prevailing custom. In any case, by 1962 average bonus was being paid at most times when men were not on piecework. One key exception was the circumstances in which a man applied to have his job value 'reobserved'—a process which is likely to lead to an increase in earnings. The financial disincentive to easy applications for 'reobservations' was seen to be so important by management that in that year they took the unprecedented step of negotiating a written agreement with the stewards. This 'Reobservation Agreement' included the sentences: 'Average bonus will not be paid up to the time that agreement has been reached but such additional time will apply to the whole batch (i.e. retrospective payment on the basis of the job value finally agreed). If, however, any experimental work or alteration in method is required by the foreman in settling the additional time, such work would be the subject of an extra allowance.'

Although the agreement is unambiguous on this point, it appears that in the following years it was increasingly ignored. If questioned about their liberality the foremen would have probably argued that there was a minor alteration in method that could be squeezed past under the second sentence quoted. In any case, within four years it appears that the payment of average bonus in all circumstances had become commonplace.

In 1966 a dispute occurred around the matter. A man requested a reobservation of his job. His foreman was busy and unable to confirm that the claim was justified and when the ratefixer looked at the job he asserted that there could be no justification for any higher job value. The basis of the dispute was that the pieceworker had not been paid average earnings for the time he had spent waiting for, and arguing with, the ratefixer. Management's dispute records show the shop steward as claiming that 'custom and practice had been broken through not paying average bonus.'

The works manager replied that 'This (i.e. the state of affairs when the foreman is unavailable) was not discussed when the Reobservation Agreement was made five years ago. Then the number of reobservations had been very small ... now it has quadrupled. Consequently it is difficult for the foreman to get to the job. Why, in any case, should average bonus be paid?'

'Because', replies the steward, 'it has been custom and practice to do so for two years'.

In the extended argument that follows the works manager does not dispute this; but he does claim that it is not sufficient justification. In the end he is reported as saying that 'It was clear that they could put forward no other argument than "custom and practice" and although he would not personally have agreed to pay average bonus under such circumstances, unfortunately someone had done so and set a precedent and therefore he would not resist this particular claim also because he did not want to complicate a future situation when the Company were going to negotiate the suspension of the Reobservation Agreement'. He is later recorded as saying that 'he had only just discovered that average bonus was being paid at the start of the meeting.'

MANAGEMENT'S PART IN C&P CREATION

This example and subsequent ones make it clear that management is heavily implicated in the creation of C&P rules. This implication may, for simplicity's sake, be divided into two forms: errors of commission and errors of omission.

Errors of commission by management that set precedents from which C&P can grow usually take the form of concessions to workers. This is easy to appreciate where first-line supervision is involved and where the bargaining climate is like that of the last example. Here foremen will have no effective disciplinary powers over their men and must use what inducements they can to gain cooperation. The concession of, say, a generous allowance to one man for a minor favour is liable to set a precedent which will be pressed for by others in the same situation and, eventually, generalized into a local C&P rule. What started out as a minor individual reward from within the range of the foreman's discretion can easily come to stretch at and then break through his discretionary limits, establishing new transactional rules in the process.

The other sort of error of commission that stands out from the case studies is also illustrated by the last example. This arises when a senior manager intervenes in a situation where he is ignorant of day-to-day practices. It is common for a works manager to reach a settlement with the shop stewards' convenor in a moment of crisis and, because he is out of touch with the shopfloor, the works manager's settlement has consequences that he is unable to foresee. Because of this greater authority, the precedents that the more senior manager sets have considerably more substance than those set by the foreman. The higher the manager who sets the precedent for C&P, the greater its likelihood of becoming an established rule.

Managerial errors of omission are those which permit customs to become established through negligence or ignorance. A ratefixer who regularly fails to prevent workers slowing down their machines before a work study is likely to find a strike on his hands when he starts trying to dictate how fast they should be run, even if he is officially supposed to do that. A foreman who overlooks the misrecording of work or the pilfering of components for a period of time will find it difficult to tighten up his controls on these matters. Similarly, although the emergence of the 'average bonus' rule in the example was a consequence of errors of commission by foremen, the fact that the works manager had not known about this for so long was an error of omission on his part. If he had been more in touch and had intervened a couple of years earlier the C&P rule would probably never have become established. Errors of omission are primarily the consequence

of poor management information systems and deserve
further consideration later.

THE WORKERS' PART IN C&P CREATION

Implicit in the example as in all bargaining matters is the
threat that workers might use sanctions. The weak bargaining position of foremen made it difficult for them to remove
concessions once they became established. The weak bargaining position of the senior manager was so painfully
apparent to him that he was willing to back-pedal and
recognize the C&P rule on average bonus rather than face
a stoppage of work. A subsequent senior manager in the
factory precipitated a major strike when he attempted to
tighten up the interpretation of the same rule.

But it would be misleading to conclude that workers
carve out fresh C&P rules through the wilful use of their
bargaining strength. The writer met an instance in the same
factory as the last example which suggested that there was
an important restraint upon such behaviour. While he was
talking to the Convenor of stewards one of the other
stewards came in with a complaint from a member of
his section. It had been normal to pay men in the production shop the timerate earnings of the toolroom when they
were asked to do occasional one-off jobs (because of excess
work load in the toolroom). The rate for the toolroom had
fallen behind the average earnings of the man's section
and, in any case, his own normal piecework earnings were
well above that rate per hour. Did he have to do the job
and did he still have to have that rate? The Convenor
pointed to the coding on the job card and said that there was
little choice—the man was 'on thin ice' in contesting the
matter and should not 'push it too far'. The shop steward
then took the matter to the Works Manager who confirmed
that the payment was 'accepted practice' but said that, in
future, such a job would go to one of the lower earners
so that none would be penalized. This verbal (and hurried)
statement by the Works Manager was taken by the stewards

as an authoritative ruling which can be seen to introduce a new rule of inflexibility in work allocation.

The example shows that, even in a factory where workers regularly use sanctions, the shop stewards are unwilling to use this power against what they see to be an established C&P rule, however unpleasant it might be to the worker directly concerned. They accept readily enough the new rule that the works manager's hasty error (of commission) establishes, but they consider it illegitimate to, as it were, bash out fresh rules on their own.

To some observers this interpretation of shop steward behaviour may seem very naïve. Examples can be cited where stewards blatantly 'try things on' and where they endeavour to establish fresh and favourable rules by a combination of half truths and crude threats. This picture of the steward as the aggressive opportunist will receive further attention in the next chapter. Let it suffice here to say that it appears not to fit the behaviour of the great majority of shop stewards. A major reason for this is simply that the average employee does not take sanctions against his employer frivolously. If employees are moved to strike, it is usually because they feel that they have a legitimate grievance. In the context of the current discussion the grievance is likely to be that they feel management is attacking a C&P rule that they accept as being legitimate. Consequently the question that must next be asked is what makes C&P rules legitimate in the eyes of workers.

This is relatively simple to understand where the C&P originated in what has been called errors of commission by management. The authority that managers at all levels have by virtue of their office bestows some legitimacy upon all their decisions. This might be termed 'managerial legitimacy' because it derives from managerial prerogative. As has been said already, the higher the manager concerned in initiating the new C&P rule, the greater the initial legitimacy of the precedent to the workers involved. Even where it is a low-level foreman who is involved in establishing a new practice, the fact that he is 'the boss' to his men will give him authority in their eyes. When C&P rules based upon this sort of legitimacy are threatened, it is easy to see why the workers involved should have a very sincere sense of grievance.

Where managerial errors of omission are the source of the C&P, however, the basis of the grievance is more complicated. Indeed, the very fact that it is the absence of managerial involvement rather than its presence that is critical suggests that it is incorrect to refer to the practices that arise as transactional rules. They are, in the first instance, pure customs growing like mushrooms in the darkness beyond management's sight. Why is it then, that when management first glimpses them and challenges them workers consider it to be legitimate to take action in their defence?

The form of legitimacy involved here is that of habit or pure custom. It appears to be empirically the case that if people act in a certain way for a period of time they come to accept their actions as legitimate. If there is no rule to the contrary (or, at least, no effectively enforced rule) and workers have got into the habit of working in a certain way, then when that habit is challenged by management it is its 'customary legitimacy' in their eyes which gives them a sense of being wronged. If they face up to the challenge then whether the habit continues will depend upon their bargaining strength relative to management's. Once management loses or avoids the challenge then the habit will become a C&P rule because the process of management recognition will have bestowed 'managerial legitimacy' upon it. The challenge, implicit or otherwise, consummates the transactional rule. Examples will be given later in which management does face up to the challenge and the workers back down, snuffing out the customary legitimacy of the habit as they do so.

It would be misleading to suggest either that the implicit challenge is always a precise event or that the notions of 'customary' and 'managerial' legitimacy are always clearly distinguished. A custom or habit may never confront management directly as a challenge but may gradually become so obvious to all concerned that its C&P rule status is in no doubt. The last example showed how a C&P rule could emerge with workers aware of both sorts of legitimacy. For on the one hand they could appeal to the length of time that it had been accepted ('... it has been custom and practice to do so for two years') and hence to customary legitimacy. On the other hand its managerial legitimacy is also clear ('... unfortunately someone had ... set a precedent'). Further, the two may be closely linked insofar as workers will want to maintain a good working relationship with their foreman and are consequently more likely to use 'we have done it this way in the past' as a justification than to claim 'the foreman lets us do it this way'.

THE ACCEPTANCE OF C&P

Although C&P rules become widely accepted as a solid basis for working relationships between junior management and men, the attitude of senior management to them may be one of studied avoidance and disapproval. Although C&P may be pragmatically accepted as 'the way things are done' at shopfloor level, senior management may deny the legitimacy of the rules.

An example of this is given by a factory where it had been tradition for many years for pieceworkers in the machine shop to 'black' jobs on which they failed to gain an acceptable job value. Management then customarily took the jobs 'off the clock' onto time rates although they recognized that this was 'contrary to all national agreements'. In the mid-1960s management decided that 'to minimise repercussions, while not sanctioning blacking' they would not ask workers on subsequent shifts to touch blacked jobs. Consequently this became established as a C&P rule. When a new works manager arrived he tried to reverse the practice, so precipitating a series of strikes. The particular interest of the case for this discussion is that there was a difference of opinion among senior management on this. The personnel department argued that he should 'respect C&P' and that if he wanted to change the rule he should take it through procedure. The works manager refused to credit any legitimacy to what he considered a scandalous practice.

This refusal to recognize the *de facto* legitimacy of C&P rules was behind the collapse of attempts to renegotiate the engineering industry's disputes procedure agreement between the EEF and the CSEU. The particular problem on which talks stalled had long been a source of controversy: the 'status quo' clause. An interpretation of this requires a knowledge of the prevailing agreements in a workshop so that, when a dispute occurs, those concerned know the legitimate 'status quo' methods of working to revert to. During the talks Mr Scanlon (for the CSEU) gave his definition of 'established' in the context of 'established practice': '. . . i.e. that it applies to all the conditions which are the subjects of agreements between stewards and management or are hallowed, for the want of a better word, in practices which are recognized even if they are not the subject of specific agreements between stewards and management but are recognized between these two people. . . . "Established" was that which was in being either as a result of agreement in written form or "established" in the sense of a practice duly recognized by the stewards and management'.
Mr Fielding (EEF): ' "Established domestic agreements".'
Mr Scanlon: 'You use the word "agreement" again.'
Mr Fielding: 'A practice agreement?'
Mr Jukes (EEF): 'It is really a custom and practice agreement, is it not?'[9]

The discussion continued in unfruitful wrestlings with semantics for many hours. No form of words could be agreed which would reassure the two sides. The fears of the EEF were that a loose form of words would permit workers to produce bogus 'established practices' like rabbits out of a hat. The fears of the CSEU were that long standing C&P rules would be deemed not binding. With the wisdom of hind-sight one can see that this was inevitable. Unless the

[9] 'Proceedings at a Special Conference between Engineering Employers' Federation and Confederation of Shipbuilding and Engineering Unions', 16th April 1970, p. 20.

national negotiators were willing to do as British Leyland subsequently did and explicitly recognize the legitimacy of 'established custom and practice', there was no form of words that would reassure the unions.

The problem facing the national negotiators—and the problem that will increasingly face the National Industrial Relations Court—is that much of British industrial relations is not based upon 'agreements' at all. It is based upon C&P rules which are recognized by those who work with them. There is no way of telling from the outside how binding these rules are because they depend upon a sense of legitimacy and upon a balance of power that is rooted at the workplace. In the absence of constitutional arrangements for negotiating at the workplace it remains a brutal fact that the ultimate test of whether a C&P rule is legitimate is whether the workforce will use sanctions to defend it.

THE FACTORS REGULATING THE DEVELOPMENT OF C&P

This analysis has shown C&P rules to be transactional rules that arise, not from any explicit negotiations, but from a process whereby managerial error or accumulated habit establishes a practice which workers see as legitimate to defend. The rules come into being either when management unintentionally establishes fresh practices or when, on seeing that a custom has become established, management avoids or loses the challenge to existing rules that it presents.

This presents a fairly static picture of C&P development but it can be enlarged into an analysis of the factors that discourage or encourage the growth of C&P over time. On the management side the factors that will encourage C&P to emerge and flourish are those that will encourage fresh precedents and practices which the workforce will be willing to take action to defend. What might be called 'C&P drift' follows 'precedent drift' and managerial negligence. Consequently 'C&P drift' is likely to accompany poor information and control systems within management. The greater the gap between senior and junior management, the greater is likely to be the range of discretion within which junior management can generate dangerous precedents and the longer is likely to be the period in which customs can become established. Not only is poor management coordination liable to encourage irreversible precedents to thrive; it is also likely to give rise to inept interventions by senior managers.

For the workforce the characteristics that are relevant are those that will identify and preserve embryonic C&P. In broad terms this covers what might be called the 'bargaining awareness' of the workforce. By this is meant the extent to which workers and their representatives are capable of identifying issues as involving conflicts of interest and as being therefore negotiable. Another characteristic is the bargaining strength of the workforce. The next chapter will argue that organizational characteristics of the workforce are also important for the control of C&P development. Shop stewards are not primarily opportunists who seize on aberrations to push C&P forward but act rather as custodians of C&P who seek to get conformity to prevailing rules. The extent to which they enjoy success in this depends upon the operation of the shop steward body as a political institution.

But the argument is getting ahead of itself. The behaviour of shop stewards and managers towards C&P will be discussed at length in the next two chapters. For the moment it is necessary to see how the content of C&P rules changes as they 'drift'.

The directions in which custom and practice drifts

C&P rules, it has been emphasized, arise without deliberation, without explicit negotiation and without intention. Furthermore, their origins lie in apparently arbitrary managerial errors and oversights. It would be natural to conclude that the development of the content of C&P rules is similarly arbitrary and that C&P can drift in any direction.

A little further reflection, however, suggests that pressures on managers may give a consistent bias to their errors. In addition, the C&P rules that could emerge from these errors are not likely to be equally attractive to the workforce. Some may not be worth defending. A crude analogy can be made with classical genetic theory. Not only is the distribution of mutations unlikely to be random; the environment may not be suitable for many of these mutations to become established.

THE MANAGERIAL BIAS OF INDULGENCY

From what has already been said it can be deduced that, when labour forces are in a strong bargaining position and disciplinary powers are weak, management is likely to lean towards being indulgent in seeking the cooperation of workers. Junior managers, in particular, are likely to bend rules and create increasingly liberal precedents in their efforts to maintain good working relationships with their men.

The drift in C&P that results from this is particularly noticeable in the area of the rate of compensation for pieceworkers when work is not available or when their job has no value agreed for it. Even where a foreman has no power to increase the rate at which waiting time is paid, he may still make indulgent concessions. One instance met at two factories occurred where a range of compensation was permitted for different causes of hold-up. The compensation was increasingly generous the less the personal responsibility of the pieceworker concerned. In one factory a man was paid less when simply waiting for a machine to be repaired than when he was assisting the fitter to repair it. Here foremen adopted the simple expedient of giving the pieceworker a spanner to hold in order to pay him the enhanced rate. In the other case a higher rate was paid for time spent toolsetting than for time lost due to machine breakdowns. Here the wages manager remarked wistfully that although he knew that setting was a minor activity in his factory and that breakdowns were frequent, the records of lost time actually paid suggested that quite the reverse was the case. Foremen were, in fact, consistently misrecording in order to benefit their men.

In the two factories last referred to, supervision was under considerable pressure from workers. A further instance comes from one in which management control over the payment system and over the largely female labour force was close and unchallenged. One chink in this tight control system allowed a slight leeway of foreman discretion. Foremen were enabled to compensate pieceworkers for lost time at a rate that varied between the equivalent of 80 to 90 per cent of average earnings, depending upon the extent to which the worker was responsible for the hold-up. Despite the docility of the labour force, foremen said that they 'invariably' paid the full 90 per cent. The maximum rate had become customary.

Besides this tendency for supervisors to strain at the limit of their discretion, one can find a tendency for them to go considerably beyond that limit if they stand little chance of detection. The over-recording of waiting time provides an instance of this. The American sociologist Roy gives a lucid example of foreman collusion in such over-recording:

'Art (foreman) was at the time cage when I punched off the day work of reaming and on to the piecework of drilling. He came around to my machine shortly after. "Say," he said, "when you punched off your day work onto piecework you ought to have your piecework already started. Run a few : then punch off day work, and you'll have a good start. You've got to chisel a little around here to make the money." '[10]

The foreman's involvement may be more than collusion. In some instances foremen initiate the practice. One told the writer: 'What we usually do if we think a bloke's done a good job or not had a fair deal is put him down for an hour or so's allowance time'. At another factory a foreman

[10] D. F. Roy, 'Efficiency and the "Fix": Informal Intergroup Relations in a Piecework Machine Shop', *American Journal of Sociology*, 1955.

said that he could usually 'make up pay somewhere' if he felt a man had had bad luck. At another again the factory manager said that he could give men an 'out of office' payment 'to give them a decent wage if you like' if they came to him with a plausible case. The 'out of office' payments were white cards intended for use as recording waiting time but had become almost a form of private currency. So extensive was this practice at one establishment that the aggregated weekly statistical returns showed pieceworkers in some departments to have been booked for more hours waiting time than they had spent under the factory roof —and they had been booked for a full week's piecework hours on top of that.

Another area where bargaining pressure tends to make foremen increasingly liberal in compensatory payment is that which occurs when pieceworkers are transferred from the machine or job with which they are familiar to one to which they are unaccustomed. Where the labour force is passive it is sometimes possible in practice to redirect workers with no compensation for any consequent loss in earnings. But an illustration of the transition stage—to full compensation of average earnings—is given by the case where foremen were empowered to give a temporary 'learning curve' compensation. This applied for a fixed time within which the operator should have become familiar with the new job. Here it was becoming the practice to 'renew' the learning curve if it appeared that the pieceworker's earnings were not attaining their previous level, thus, in effect, guaranteeing his average earnings.

The tendency for C&P to drift in the direction of greater liberality is often accompanied by a tendency for it to become more confused and unclear to the participants. This is illustrated by the C&P rules that govern the criteria whereby jobs may be reobserved even if there has not been a change in 'materials, means or method'. As has been said, under steady inflation, jobs whose values were determined a long time ago become increasingly 'tight' and unremunerative to pieceworkers. Unless management introduces some means of increasing their values (and such means have to be very sophisticated to be effective), a rule has to be developed to make old times acceptable. The most specific rule of this kind encountered was one that decreed that a job ought to be restudied if it was more than four years old. Less precise was the rule at another factory where management said that it 'couldn't resist' revaluing a job which was more than three or four years old. But age tends to become eroded as a criterion. One factory had a major stoppage when management insisted that only 'old' jobs could be restudied although, the shop stewards maintained, it had become C&P to restudy 'bad paying' jobs. They maintained that over the years it had become common for foremen to revalue jobs solely on account of the relatively poor earnings of their operators and irrespective of the date on which their value had been agreed. The views of the participants bore out the general confusion as to criteria. A foreman said the criterion was 'if it's five years old'; the senior ratefixer, 'if the pieceworker can't make his money'; a shop steward, 'anything more than three years old'. An inspection of the actual dates upon which piecework values in the factory were last agreed reflected the looseness of the rules; half of them were more than five years old and a third more than nine years.

When C&P rules drift further still, time may become abandoned as a criterion for reobservation. Thus at one factory the plant superintendent said that jobs were revalued when the men 'were getting no more out of the job' and when 'all the slack in the job times was gone' and his colleague the senior ratefixer said that there were 'no set rules'. In these circumstances the main criterion is comparison between the earnings of the individual whose job is in question and those of his fellow pieceworkers. Sometimes these comparisons are effectively restricted to the particular section in which the individual works—comparison with earnings elsewhere in the factory is rejected. Sometimes there is no such qualification; a job can be revalued if its earnings are, simply, 'unreasonably low'.

All this suggests that many of the precedents and errors of commission initiated by management are biased towards being indulgent towards workers. Junior managers and foremen are especially willing to bend rules within the limits of their accountability or identifiability to their seniors. Since C&P rules that originate in this way are likely to be very acceptable to workers, it is highly likely that workers will defend them against any subsequent efforts by management to remove them.

THE WORKERS' BIAS TOWARDS UNILATERAL CONTROL

Discussions of workshop bargaining often note the high degree of unilateral job regulation that workers come to exercise. But it is usually unclear how they come to acquire this control or how deliberately it was acquired. An examination of the growth of C&P provides some answers to these questions in the case of piecework.

There are many signs that C&P drifts towards increasing worker control over work. It is evident, for instance, in the matter of the procedure followed in estimating and negotiating piecework values. C&P rules tend to develop to restrict the freedom with which management selects operators to be work studied. They come to prevent the selection of the notorious fast worker (or 'greyhound') because studies of him might lead to 'tight' piecework values becoming established. They tend to develop to inhibit refinements to work study technique (such as the use of stop watches) presumably because these strengthen management's hand in negotiation. Similarly, they develop to prevent demonstrations by management which might prove 'tight' values to be technically feasible. This sort of restriction on management, by weighting the balance of the bargain in the pieceworker's favour, increases the chance that the outcome of the bargain will be 'fair' and predictable to the worker. As will be discussed in the next chapter, the reduction of the uncertainty with which one has to work is a very widespread aim of worker action.

It is of particular interest that this drift of C&P rules (in such a way that they increase workers' control over their earnings) increases, as an incidental side product, workers' control over other aspects of their work. Consider, for instance, the mobility of workers between jobs or departments. C&P rules may develop that severely restrict this mobility. An example of a dispute over the content of these rules is given by the record of a management complaint to its factory's shop steward committee:

'Some 12 months ago we wanted to transfer labour in the fitting shop . . . under a C&P arrangement. The fitters demanded average bonus and someone turned up a grubby piece of paper, made in 1947 when we were producing (only) four machines per period, and said that the gangs must have a voice in any compilation of gangs. Here was a case where we asked people to be sensible and accept a custom and practice agreement. This attitude goes some way towards committing industrial suicide.' Behind this dispute lay the fact that different gangs had different levels of earnings and the fear on the part of the workers that they could be transferred to a lower earning gang. The fitters won this particular dispute.

Another example concerns the control of the 'feeds and speeds' at which lathes are run. These determine the rate at which metal is cut away from the material being worked. The 'feed' is the rate at which the cutting tool traverses and the 'speed' is the rate at which the metal is driven against it. Excessive feeds and speeds are liable to damage the tool and produce a poor finish. Their correct calculation is a matter for fine technical judgement and is normally done by production engineers or their equivalent although skilled men will also be competent where their own work is concerned.

There are two particular aspects of the matter on which C&P rules tend to develop to give pieceworkers control over feeds and speeds. One, of particular relevance to semi-skilled workers, is that the machine is set at a particular feed and speed by management and the operators often attempt illicitly to increase this to enhance their earnings. The second is that ratefixers attempt to study the piecework job at the correct feed and speed but are forced, by bargaining pressure from the workers, to do so at a slower one. Once the piecework value has been agreed the worker promptly increases the feed and speed of his lathe with consequent gain in earnings.

On the first of these aspects an example can be given of the successful establishment of a C&P rule that gave semi-skilled workers substantial control over feeds and speeds. This occurred in a factory where there was no tradition of concerted industrial action over piecework matters. On this occasion, however, a foreman put a lock and chain on the regulator of the machine of a man whom he considered to be a regular offender at speeding up. The whole factory came to a standstill with an immediate strike and the foreman was forced to remove the lock. Although he said that he did so 'in good faith' that machines would not be speeded up again he also admitted his being unable to prevent it, saying: 'You can't get a man for doing it when you find him because they all do it.' It was generally felt that this incident had strengthened into a C&P rule the control over their machines that semi-skilled workers had established as a custom.

The second aspect—the control of feeds and speeds at the time that the job is being studied before a value is agreed on it—is illustrated by an unsuccessful attempt to confirm a possible C&P rule. The factory involved here experienced intensive bargaining and frequent stoppages. At a Works Conference the stewards maintained that 'operators say that they have a right to fix feeds and speeds . . . they consider that they are sufficiently skilled to know what feeds and speeds are required on each job. They have done this so long that it is custom and practice.' The plant manager replied that 'this was incorrect, it had never been considered custom and practice, in fact the Company had evidence that ratefixers had asked operators to raise feeds and speeds during studies; this had happened on many occasions.'

The ensuing argument moved on to the earnings level of the workers involved and to the fact that they wanted feeds and speeds in their control so that they could avoid 'tight' values on jobs. But, even though this was recognized as the root of the problem, the bulk of the argument is still over the matter of control. The shop stewards maintained that 'the Company is saying that it has the right to fix feeds and speeds to be used during a study'.

'We are not saying that,' replied the plant manager; 'what we are saying is that we have the right to ask the operator to perform at another feed and speed. Naturally, if the operator considers one feed to be satisfactory and the ratefixer another, it might be necessary to ask the foreman to arbitrate. The books of the National and Local Agreements state clearly that the time settlement should be mutual.'

The concluding stages saw the Company re-emphasizing its position that 'neither side had the absolute right to determine a feed or speed. . . . It could never be accepted that it was the sole right of the man to establish the feeds and speeds while a time study was being taken. . . . The Company were insisting on the right to have a voice in the setting of feeds and speeds which it regarded as custom and practice.'

As has been said, management was here successful in suppressing a custom that was hindering the ratefixers and in preventing it becoming established C&P. Even so, the C&P rule that was reconfirmed in its stead gave far less to managerial prerogative than many managements would admit. The record of the dispute demonstrates how monetary matters can become apparently inextricably entangled with wider questions of the control of work. The pursuit of more stable and predictable earnings led to workers in the examples gaining control over their mobility between gangs and over the speeds at which their machines were run.

From the earlier analysis of the development of C&P it can be seen that it requires no conspiracy to explain how workers acquire unilateral control over job regulation. It is simply that management errors that enhance the control that individual workers have over their earnings are more likely to be used as precedents for C&P than those that do not. Such mutations will find themselves in a friendly environment and will serve the short-term goals of individual workers who want to stabilize their earnings. The wider implications for the control of matters such as mobility and machine speeds will probably not be considered at the time. This implies that workers gain unilateral control of job regulation in some areas almost by accident and certainly not by design. This is a paradoxical implication and begs an obvious question about the role of shop stewards in the process. Consideration of that must wait until the next chapter.

THE UNIFORMITY OF C&P DRIFT

If it is the case, as has been suggested, that C&P rules drift in certain predictable directions in piecework systems, how uniform is this drift? Do they drift on a broad front, so that if a piecework system is worker-generous in one rule it is likely to be similarly worker-generous in others? Or is it the case that, because C&P arises from haphazard errors and without strategic intention, there is unlikely to be any correlation between the extent to which different C&P rules have drifted?

From what has already been said, there are two reasons for favouring the view that they drift on a broad front. In the first place the pattern of rules regulating a piecework system appears in some respects to act like an integrated system. It has been shown how pressure to increase workers' control of earnings may generate drift in rules ostensibly unconnected with money. Secondly, it has been argued that the factors that regulate the rate of C&P drift in a plant are connected with management control systems and the political organization of the workforce. Since these factors are, superficially at any rate, equally germane for all C&P it implies that C&P would be expected to drift fairly uniformly.

TABLE 4:1

The index of C&P leniency and its components

Area covered by transactional rule	A	B	C	D	E	F	G	H	J	K
Criteria for job reobservation	5	4	4	2	3	4	5	1	2	1
Compensation for mobility	5	3	3	2	3	3	4	1	1	2
Operator control of 'feeds and speeds'	5	5	5	1	3	3	5	1	1	1
Waiting time payment	4	3	4	3	3	3	4	2	2	1
Payment when no job value	5	3	5	3	3	3	5	1	1	1
Restrictions on work study	4	4	5	2	2	5	4	1	1	1
Mean—Index of C&P leniency	4·7	3·7	4·3	2·2	2·8	3·5	4·5	1·2	1·3	1·2
Mean deviation from mean	0·4	0·7	0·7	0·6	0·3	0·7	0·5	0·3	0·4	0·3
Average annual compound increase in standard earnings from non-negotiated drift—as in Table 2:1	5·0	4·8	5·1	3·1	4·5	5·0	6·5	1·8	2·1	1·2
Topsy factor	83	78	81	57	66	77	81	20	45	35

may not sometimes indicate that a "spontaneous" demonstration will help to secure or expedite a settlement. Although on the whole, the stewards here appear as attempting to minimize trouble; but when trouble seems inevitable, they attempt to assert their leadership, in order to maintain their authority over the operatives.'[21] Clack adds that 'In short, the convenors and shop steward organization at the factory did not appear as a driving force behind labour unrest, but could more validly be regarded as "shock absorbers" of the industrial relations machinery'.[22]

Although these findings of Turner and his colleagues have been important and influential in correcting the 'trouble-maker' picture of the steward that is so widely held, it would be misleading to ignore the evidence that stewards do sometimes provoke and organize strikes in a deliberate way. Such evidence is provided by the minute book of the closely integrated stewards' committee at factory B:

> 'The convenor stated that it was becoming more and more difficult to achieve wage applications through the normal negotiating procedure and he appealed to the membership, if their claim were justifiable, they must support their claim by a show of militance, bearing in mind, to keep in touch with the Shop Stewards' Committee at all times.'

The background here is one in which management is attempting to tighten up on the criteria whereby piece-workers can get jobs revalued. What is seen by the stewards to be a C&P procedural rule is being eroded and, since steward representations have had no effect, they see no alternative but to demonstrate to management that the breaking of a procedural 'agreement' will be countered by stoppages and disorders on the shopfloor.

Other clear instances of shop steward inspired strikes came, at factory B, when management tried to cut back on the time allowed off (mainly through custom) for meetings

[21] Turner *et al.*, *op. cit.*, p. 214.
[22] G. Clack, *Industrial Relations in a British Car Factory*, Cambridge: Cambridge University Press, 1967, p. 91.

F

of the Joint Shop Stewards' Committee and when, as quoted
from the minutes earlier, the ratefixers started timing new
recruits contrary to a C&P rule. There is also an example
from factory A. Despite its poorly integrated shop steward
committee, when management tried to tighten up the
criteria whereby 'old' jobs could be revalued (and thus
reverse a C&P rule) it was the senior stewards who spread
the word and organized the stoppage.

What is common to these examples is that shop stewards
are precipitating strikes in order to defend what they see to
be established C&P rules. They are mobilizing the collective strength of their workforces in their role as 'the principal guardians of C&P'.

It is worthwhile drawing out the distinction implied by
Turner, Clack and Roberts when they talked of 'unofficial-
unofficial' strikes. The sort of stoppage they meant by this
—one in which the steward was brought in after the walk-
out had occurred and did not foment it—was common at
most of the case study factories in which the workforces
had a fairly high level of 'bargaining awareness'. At some
it was regularly used in the later stages of a piecework
bargain. Some stoppages were of the type described by Clack
as 'downers' which 'were "attention getters" rather than
actions to obtain general economic concessions'. Of the latter
the tacit approval of the foreman concerned was sometimes
so obvious when, for example, the section ran short of raw
material, that the outside observer could not help but see
brief, sectional stoppages as an essential part of the management information system.

The 'unofficial-unofficial' strike appeared to be more
frequent in workforces where bargaining awareness was high
but shop steward integration was low. By contrast, the
steward inspired strike in defence of C&P rules can be
termed 'official-unofficial'. This is the sort of sanction used
by stewards to further the broader, more strategic objectives
of a more centralized organization. The other important use
of the 'official-unofficial' strike besides that of protecting
C&P is in supporting the central negotiations that the

steward body has with management. By using this form of action an integrated shop steward body shows itself to be, not a collection of industrial eunuchs, but a sophisticated political organization capable of making the most efficient use of the bargaining power of the workforce.

THE NEGOTIATED ALTERNATIVE TO C&P DRIFT

It is now possible to resolve the paradox raised earlier, that the more integrated a shop steward body becomes so the more it tends to choke off the C&P drift which superficially appears to give it both wider powers and more generous 'agreements'. For stewards cannot influence the direction of C&P drift with any certainty. Furthermore, any attempts they might make to do so are likely to reduce their authority with both workers and management. Such attempts are likely to require workers to take collective action over weakly-held and tendentious grievances and they are likely to damage seriously the existing bargaining relationships with management. This is not to say that stewards do not 'try it on' and drum up feeling over tongue-in-cheek grievances. They often do, and the circumstances in which they do so will be discussed in the next section. What is being argued is that opportunistic attempts to provoke C&P drift will be contrary to the objects of an integrated shop steward body and are likely to be discouraged by it.

An integrated shop steward body develops a predilection for explicit negotiation with management. In doing this it can engage in the creation of fresh rules of job regulation in a deliberate, intentional way and can deploy its sanctions economically and with maximum effect. By formalizing plant level negotiations management effectively deepens the recognition it gives to its employees' trade union organization. It reinforces the procedural position of the stewards and, if any plant agreements negotiated between them are written down, the stewards' position is reinforced further.[23]

[23] The process of formalizing plant bargaining and the impact of this upon shop stewards is discussed at length in Department of Employment, Manpower Papers No 5, *The Reform of Collective Bargaining at Plant and Company Level*, London: HMSO, 1971.

Discussion of productivity agreements has tended to
characterize the shift to formality within a factory's bargaining system as a sharp change. This is misleading. Although
an integrated shop steward body will have a predisposition
to negotiate centrally with management in a formal way,
it may be able to do so only on a limited range of subjects.
In most of the establishments studied there was a considerable amount of formal and centralized negotiation going
on alongside C&P drift. The issues on which these two
modes of rule determination took place differed. Such
matters as working hours, discipline and short-time working procedure generally appear to get transferred to the
arena of formal negotiation before such matters as flexibility
of working, compensation for lost time and piecework bargaining procedures.

Because this study has been concerned with piecework
bargaining it has necessarily concentrated upon non-
negotiated rules. Piecework systems offer fertile fields for
C&P growth. The increasing formalization of bargaining,
however, is accompanied by the transfer of issues from the
non-negotiated to the negotiated 'sector'. It is often difficult to evaluate how far this process has proceeded. In
particular, it is often difficult to identify whether a written
agreement is, as it appears, the outcome of a formal negotiation between managers and the stewards' committee, or
whether it is merely a 'consolidation' agreement which
records the current state of C&P in the factory. The
former of these would be the deliberate creation of fresh
rules to overcome some current problem. The latter would
be a passive act. If prosecuted with energy such an act
might 'freeze' C&P drift and provide stable agreements.
But often such agreements become neglected and provide
no more than a snapshot of a past pattern of C&P which
has subsequently become overlaid by further drift.

There is a deliberate and obvious analogy to be drawn
between the analysis of rules of job regulation given here
and the analysis of forms of wage drift developed in previous
chapters. In principle it might be possible to produce a

Topsy factor for rules of job regulation; this would indicate the proportion of new rules that emerged over a period of time through non-negotiated as opposed to negotiated processes. In this case a high Topsy factor would mean that only a small proportion of rules arose from formal negotiation. It would imply that the integration of the shop steward body was low.

One further point should be made about the shift to formal workshop negotiation. It has been shown that C&P tends to drift in such a way that rules go straight from unilateral management regulation to unilateral worker regulation. It is difficult for C&P drift to create rules of joint worker/management regulation. This is because joint regulation is a relatively sophisticated political solution that usually requires explicit negotiations between recognised representatives of the two sides. Thus, by opting for greater formality, a shop steward body opts for more joint regulation.

This may seem perverse, insofar as it is often assumed, certainly from the workers' point of view and probably from that of the stewards also, that the unilateral control of work by workers is necessarily preferable to them to its joint regulation. But this ignores the complexity of most work organisations. The control of individual jobs by workers when they do not also have control of the broader coordination of those jobs can lead to situations which are very unsatisfactory from their point of view. It is not necessarily the case that the loss of control by one side leads to its gain by the other. It is commonplace to find situations in which no-one has control. An example is provided by the productivity bargains in the fuel distribution industry.[24] Before the bargains took place men had a considerable degree of unilateral control over their jobs but had to work sixty hours a week to earn an acceptable wage. Because the work was organized inefficiently and because the workers used time-

[24] This is described and analysed in National Board for Prices and Incomes, Report No 36, *Productivity Agreements*, Cmnd. 3311, London: HMSO, 1967.

wasting practices, it was found possible through the productivity bargains to do the same work for the same wage in only forty hours. Unilateral control of a small area was exchanged for joint control of a much larger one. Put another way, joint control is usually preferable to inadequate control.

FACTORS CONTROLLING THE DEGREE OF INTEGRATION

So far this chapter has developed a hypothesis of shop steward organization and has argued that the form of this organization is important for the development of C&P rules in particular and for the conduct of industrial relations in general.[25] The hypothesis suggests that, as a workforce becomes increasingly aware of bargainable issues and provided it has some power over management, there are two alternative routes along which shop steward development can take place. On the one hand, the shop steward body can move towards closer integration. This will be accompanied by the more sparing and more effective use of sanctions, by improving bargaining relationships and by pressure for formal centralized negotiations. On the other hand the steward body may move the other way. In this case there will be faster C&P drift, more uncoordinated use of sanctions, higher shop steward turnover, more opportunist stewards, deteriorating bargaining relationships and broadening criteria on what constitutes a strikeable grievance.

This picture is of necessity simplified, but its implications for the conduct of piecework bargaining are so far-reaching that this study would be incomplete without some

[25] There were not adequate data available on the degree of shop steward integration for any quantitative tests to be carried out of the hypothesis developed in the previous sections. A contrast of factories A and B, where bargaining awareness and power appeared to be similar but integration of stewards was very different, can be made. The respective indices for C&P leniency for A and B were 4·7 and 3·7 and the Topsy factors (over the extended period 1954 to 1970) were respectively 81 per cent and 72 per cent. These results are fully consistent with the hypothesis.

discussion of the factors that influence shop steward integration. Why is it that some shop steward organizations become increasingly integrated while others remain uncoordinated and feeble?

It is commonly remarked upon by managers and stewards that the strong personalities of individuals are important in keeping the stewards' committee on a sound constitutional footing, and in concentrating power in it. Apart from the unsatisfactory nature of this explanation from the point of view of social scientists—for it is difficult to make useful generalizations from it—it does not explain how traditions of constitutionality and of a high level of integration can remain strong within a workforce for decade after decade. For it appears that once a steward body has reached a certain stage of integration it can accommodate strong and weak leaderships and palace revolutions among senior stewards without disintegrating. Personalities may be important as catalysts in the first instance, but they do little to explain the continuing pattern of behaviour.

The trade union organizations outside the factory do not appear to help with an explanation either. In the factories studied the national unions had sometimes been important in an initial recruiting drive but it proved difficult for them to guide the development of the shop steward organization after that. Some stewards were grateful for the advice and encouragement that they had received from their local full-time officers. Others (especially those who had been involved in starting their organization twenty or so years ago) said that the full-time officers could provide little help.

More satisfactory explanations must be sought on the management side. The shift towards formal bargaining in an establishment traditionally dominated by C&P requires the shop steward leadership to take initiatives that involve considerable risks to its electoral position. Its willingness to take these risks in establishing a stable bargaining relationship depends very much upon how far management assists it. This assistance will have to be very much more political than merely providing a desk, telephone, check-off system, time for meetings and so on. In some of the factories studied, rapid changes in management personnel and policy had made a stable relationship impossible. Where such a relationship was being built successfully the important factors appeared to be whether the manager primarily concerned had the power to prevent his decisions being over-ridden by his colleagues and whether he had the diplomatic ability to support the senior stewards and help them save face with their members when they made mistakes.

The control that management has over itself is a major factor determining the integration of the shop steward body. For anything that increases the chances of discordant precedents being set increases the difficulties confronting stewards who are trying to coordinate their workforce. Consider, for example, the position of a senior steward who has put his name to a formally negotiated agreement when he is called into a dispute over a C&P rule in one department of the factory. He discovers not only that the C&P rule in question conflicts with the formal agreement but also that the workers concerned have good reason for considering the rule to be legitimate because it had become established through a series of errors by their foreman. If the steward defends the C&P rule he upsets the agreement and the relationship with management; if he helps management to obliterate the C&P rule he loses the support of a part of the workforce and weakens the steward committee. Weak management control systems are likely to present senior stewards who are involved in formal plant bargaining with continuing embarassment.

Weak control systems also make formal central negotiation difficult by making a coherent management industrial relations policy impossible. Any central negotiation is likely to become undermined if the various supervisors within the factory continue to operate as independent policy makers. An inadequate disputes procedure is likely to bring similar trouble. For it will encourage lower management to make short-cuts by reaching informal agreements that set fresh precedents for C&P. It is also likely to increase ill-informed interventions by senior managers with the same result.

Finally, there is the general question of the writing down of agreements. McCarthy[26] has discussed at some length the reasons for managements' reluctance to commit the results of workshop bargaining to paper. This is felt to make concessions irreversible and to reinforce the procedural status of shop stewards. It also widens the base from which it is felt fresh encroachments upon management prerogatives can be made. It makes apparent to senior management and possibly to the public that these prerogatives are not as intact as might be expected. McCarthy notes that 'it is . . . extremely significant that in general (shop stewards) . . . do not seek to deny that their *influence and status would in some way be advanced by a measure of codification.*'[27] There can be no doubt that the ambiguity and misunderstandings that result from unwritten C&P rules and 'gentlemen's agreements' are themselves a rich source of C&P growth.

All this suggests that, in the long run, management itself is the most important influence in shaping the behaviour of its shop stewards. The next chapter will study the characteristics of management more closely.

[26] W. E. J. McCarthy, *The Role of Shop Stewards in British Industrial Relations*, Royal Commission Research Paper, London: HMSO, 1967.
[27] *ibid.*, p. 27.

6

Management and Topsy

The Role of Management

It was demonstrated earlier that C&P rules governing piece-work bargaining tend to 'drift' across a spectrum, becoming increasingly lenient and generous towards workers. While a powerful and perceptive workforce can consolidate and defend C&P development, the incidents which actually move it forward are managerial errors. On the one hand errors of commission by management become accepted as fresh precedents while, on the other, errors of omission overlook the aberrations that result and permit them to become established as fresh C&P rules.

The behaviour of management is important to the way piecework operates in another way. Not only do managers influence the overall rules of bargaining, they also influence the conduct and outcome of individual bargains. The most obvious illustration of this is given by the support that the main-line supervision provides for work study engineers. Without this support the engineers are placed in such a weak bargaining position with respect to the workers that the work study basis of the payment system is likely to collapse altogether.

The central factor regulating management's behaviour in both these respects is that of the management control system. Different parts of management—such as foremen, production engineers, accountants, ratefixers, quality controllers and so on—tend to pursue such different objectives that their pursuit of them can easily conflict. In the jargon of management scientists, they tend to suboptimise.[1] The success of a management control system can be judged by the extent to which it prevents this, by the extent to which different management functions are constrained from acting contrary to one another and contrary to the declared objectives of the whole organization.

It is convenient to consider the significance of management control systems for piecework bargaining in two parts. For this a distinction can be drawn between line and staff management. Line managers run up from first-line supervisors, usually called foremen, through superintendents to posts such as factory manager. They are usually held accountable for the utilization of resources which means, essentially, getting the correct product made on time. Staff managers are there mainly to advise and they come under functions such as ratefixing, work study, planning, production engineering, quality control and industrial relations. The first area of controls to receive attention is the vertical one down the line. The second is the horizontal one relating line to staff and staff to itself.

THE MAIN LINE OF SUPERVISION

The rules that regulate a management system were discussed in detail by the American sociologist Gouldner. He noted that if a foreman operates under very close controls from higher management he is largely protected from pressures from the workers under him. If he is able to say that his superiors give him no possible 'leeway' within which to make concessions to workers, they are unlikely to press for them. In Gouldner's words the rules associated with an effective management control system 'largely serve to mitigate tensions *derivative* of "close supervision" rather than to remove all the major tensions which *create* it. Indeed, the rules now

---

[1] 'Suboptimizing' is defined as 'the behaviour of sub-systems which endeavour to optimize the achievement of their own limited objectives to the detriment of the (overall) system'. R. I. Tricker, *The Accountant in Management*, London: Batsford, 1967, p. 406.

make close supervision feasible.'[2] Conversely, the greater the
'leeway' within which the foreman can operate to reward
workers, the greater the pressure that those workers are likely to exert to get him to stretch at the limits of his discretion. The situation where management controls are weak
brings about a pattern of supervisory behaviour that
Gouldner calls the 'indulgency pattern'[3] which is characterized by a lenient approach to workers, a tendency to
cover up for their mistakes, to give them a second chance in
disciplinary matters and so on.

In most of the factories involved in the current study the
management control systems (if they deserve so grand
a name) became established at a time when foremen had,
and used, the power to discipline and sack men. Under high
employment and collective bargaining this power had
largely vanished. In these changed circumstances and without the support of close controls, foremen were forced to
err towards indulgency in attempting to gain the cooperation of their men. Examples of this were given in the discussion of the growth of C&P in Chapter Four.

To avoid pressures from the workers, line management
in these circumstances also tends to hand large areas of job
regulation over to shop stewards for their unilateral control. It is not difficult to see how this can happen with foremen. In his study of the Fawley refinery Flanders gave a
clear illustration of the process whereby foremen eased their
task by surrendering the allocation and control of overtime
to the stewards.[4] But it can also be senior managers
who bring stewards into positions hitherto covered by
managerial prerogatives. An illustration of this comes from
the minute books of factory B where a dispute had
developed because an inexperienced worker had accepted a

[2] A. W. Gouldner, *Patterns of Industrial Bureaucracy*, Glencoe: Free
Press, 1954, p. 177.

[3] A. W. Gouldner, *Wildcat Strike*, New York: Antioch Press,
1954, p. 18.

[4] A. Flanders, *The Fawley Productivity Agreements*, London: Faber,
1964, p. 235.

reduction in his job value for a reason that was contrary to established C&P. The record continues:

> The important point was that the shop stewards should impress on the operators never to accept a cut or a retime without consulting them ... The Convenor, who had discussed the position with (the Works Manager) stated that in future they agreed that any alteration or revision of times would only take place through joint consultation with the shop steward on the section concerned.

Subsequent records at the factory show that this verbal agreement was enforced by the stewards. An illustration of managerial acquiescence comes from a larger establishment where the factory manager freely admitted that shop stewards worked so closely with the supervision that they (the stewards) had complete control over the recording of work and wages ('since they are elected for this') leaving the foremen to look after the flow of tools and materials ('They dovetail together in their own amicable arrangements'). He felt this was an admirable arrangement because, after all, he said, 'I don't want to get involved' so long as they make sure they 'keep the gaffer happy' and so long as 'I get the right quality and don't pay too much'.

The relationship between foreman and shop steward is a complex one involving a high degree of reciprocity. Each helps the other carry out his tasks and for each one their mutual bargaining relationship is important. To senior managers and workers alike this can sometimes appear to verge on illicit collusion. The NBPI noted that foremen sometimes administered the 'banks' of completed piecework for their men in order to stabilize their earnings and that 'in stable groups foremen apparently are able to carry out some of the representative functions of shop stewards.'[5] At the other extreme it was noticeable that at some of the factories with low bargaining awareness the foremen used stewards as they might use chargehands. At factory D, for

[5] NBPI, Report No 65, *op. cit.*, p. 92. Further light is cast upon this relationship by L. Klein, *op. cit.*, and T. Lupton, *op. cit.*

instance, when they found groups of women pieceworkers using ceilings of output restriction, the foremen involved used their stewards to 'put the poison in' by encouraging the women to compete amongst each other and, in this way, they broke up the group restrictions. It is difficult to generalize about these matters other than to say that when control systems over foremen are weak their actions are governed by their bargaining strength vis-à-vis their workers.

However weak the control system over line-management's objectives is, it is usually the case that there is some control over the level of production. So long as work leaves his department on schedule the foreman can afford to ignore problems of labour costs and unsavoury precedents. Kuhn gives a case that illustrates this well.

> (The foreman) valued a workable relationship with (the lay union representative) above the lower labor loading costs on the tread-loading job and tacitly conspired with (the representative) to get a higher piece-rate. Production was so important to line management that it was willing to countenance (the foreman's) violation of the rule regarding the overloading of the tuber even though violations created precedents and would undermine the goal of industrial relations to secure uniform practices in the plant and to establish clearly defined work rules.[6]

Management's difficulties do not arise only because its control systems cover too narrow a range of objectives, however. The controls are often deficient in providing senior management with the information it requires to know what is going on at shop-floor level. On a wide range of issues—and, for this discussion, most notably in industrial relations issues—there is a gulf of ignorance between senior management and foremen. This gulf is often tacitly dredged further by those at both ends of the line of supervision. To top managers, if they have an inkling of what is going on, it may seem best to leave the informal bargaining to be looked after by those on the shop-floor for fear that too close a scrutiny of it would strengthen the procedural position of

[6] J. W. Kuhn, *op. cit.*, p. 76.

stewards. For the foremen, as Kuhn notes: 'The less that higher management, the industrial relations department, and the restriction of collective agreements are involved in his shop affairs, the freer the foreman is; the fewer grievances that go to the top, the less the notice the shop receives.'[7]

From the point of view of C&P rule creation, the gulf of ignorance within the line of supervision is of great importance. Apart from increasing the leeway within which foremen can make precedents, it also decreases the likelihood that these will be discovered and rectified before the workforce has come to accept them as established C&P. Where domestic disputes procedures are inadequate (as was the case in most of the factories studied) the chances of fresh C&P being created become still greater. For when relations between foremen and stewards temporarily break down and the senior manager intervenes, typically to cope with a stoppage, his dealings with the better-informed stewards are very likely to result in a fresh C&P rule that pushes forward further the frontiers of worker control.

THE RELATIONSHIP BETWEEN LINE AND STAFF

The inherent conflict between line and staff management has been described in detail by Dalton who concluded that 'As method refiners and technique formulators, the staffs are really specialists in change and reorganization. Sworn to stable technology, line people see changes as interfering with production.'[8] How far these different approaches can be reconciled—and also how far different staff functions can be reconciled with one another—depends upon the control system within which they all operate. A large number of control systems can exist side-by-side in a factory; controls over stocks, production, quality, cost, capital expendi-

---

[7] *ibid.*, p. 118. This does not, of course, conflict with the quote from Gouldner in the previous section. The tensions which create close supervision also tend to break up friendly reciprocity relationships.

[8] M. Dalton, *Men Who Manage*, New York: Wiley, 1959, p. 75.

ture, wages, effort, time-keeping and disputes are some of the more obvious.

It is possible to integrate most of these separate controls into an overall system. Factory H achieved this well with a 'standard cost' accounting system that related a very detailed weekly departmental report covering scores of different indicators to a rolling annual plan. When, for instance, scrap, absenteeism or payment for waiting time rose above the projected target the foreman involved would have to present plausible reasons to his works manager. But most of the factories studied (partly for technological reasons) fell far short of this and concentrated on controlling for production levels and quality to the exclusion of most other matters.

The NBPI's report saw this to be central to an understanding of where piecework pay systems tend to go awry:

> Our studies suggest that the 'demoralization' of a PBR system is not usually the consequence of a poor work study or ratefixing department as such, but of pressure from other management objectives. It usually arises because too low a priority is given to the integrity of an establishment's payment system by top management itself. The most important pressure comes from the main line of supervision. It is generally the foremen who allocate jobs, handle workplace labour relations in the first instance, deal with 'make-up' pay for lost time, and so on. Their attitude to the ratefixer or work study engineer thus largely governs his authority. The foreman's first job is to produce the right product to time and he will, not unnaturally, tend to subordinate other functions to this, if he is not given a complimentary interest in the proper use of work study, the control of costs and the integrity of the payment system.[9]

This is illustrated clearly by Kuhn:

> In the setting of piecework rates . . . the foremen are more vulnerable to fractional bargaining tactics than the time-study staff. Foremen want to maintain full production in their departments and to keep stable relations with their

[9] NBPI, Report No 65, *op. cit.*, para 185.

men. A loose rate may penalise the company by increasing labor costs or may hurt the time-study man by revealing his ineptitude, but it does not bother the foreman particularly. (He quotes a foreman as saying) 'I'll ask the time-study to fix up a rate if it's not right. Now, what's right is elastic. We have to get out a large quantity of goods. You got to throw the workers a bone. If they only make a half-hour bonus in eight, they're not going to break necks to get production out. I like to see them get a couple of minutes bonus on every piece. It pays for me in the long run. I get the job done two or three weeks earlier. I try to point out to the time-study what we lose in these tight rates. But whether you get the rate changed depends on the time-study man. He's got to understand your problem. You get an inexperienced man and it is easy to clobber him and get what you want.'[10]

Although supervision is the branch of management most often at loggerheads with the work study engineers, other staff functions can also undermine their position. If production enginers alter a method or machine without notifying them it is likely that an irreversible wage anomaly will result. If those responsible for planning give the work study engineers inadequate notice of a change in product the consequent rush can lead to an excess of 'slack' piecework values.

In a more negative way there are departments of management which should reinforce work study and hence the piecework system but often fail to do so. Inadequate cost accountancy and wage control are obvious examples. A less obvious one that appeared to be important at two factories was the department responsible for tendering for new contracts. The estimate that this department made of the likely direct labour cost per component was well known by the work study engineers and they used it as an upper limit during their bargains with pieceworkers. But, since the tendering department were mainly concerned that the actual cost of components should not exceed their original estimates (and since they were operating in relative-

[10] J. W. Kuhn, *op. cit.*, p. 92.

ly uncompetitive industries) these estimates of labour costs assumed a most pessimistically high level of inflation. Far from being a restraint on work study engineers in their bargains, the estimates positively encouraged them in a cheerful generosity towards workers' demands.

A SIMPLE TEST

The argument that poor management control systems are a cause of C&P drift and hence of a high level of non-negotiated wage drift can be strengthened by a quantitative test.

TABLE 6:1

Indicators of Management Controls

CONTROL AREA	FACTORY									
	A	B	C	D	E	F	G	H	J	K
1. Misrecording of waiting time	5	4	5	2	3	4	5	1	1	1
2. Foreman's latitude to compensate for lost time	5	3	5	3	3	5	5	1	1	1
3. Direct labour cost controls on principal bargainer	5	3	4	3	3	4	5	1	1	2
Crude average	5·0	3·3	4·7	2·7	3·0	4·3	5·0	1·0	1·0	1·3
Index of C&P 'leniency'	4·7	3·7	4·3	2·2	2·8	3·5	4·5	1·2	1·3	1·2
Topsy factor	83	79	81	57	65	77	81	20	45	35

1. *Misrecording of waiting time*
   1. None at all.
   2. Occasional but not substantial.
   3. Regular but small scale (less than 5 per cent of all hours).
   4. Extensive in some areas (less than 20 per cent of all hours).
   5. Extensive and extreme (more than 20 per cent of all hours) and with foreman collusion.
2. *Foreman's latitude to compensate for lost time*
   1. Strictly defined limits related directly to hours lost.
   3. Regular 'unofficial' compensation for cooperation.
   5. Free use of waiting time irrespective of justification in order to compensate for shortfalls in earnings.
3. *Direct labour cost controls on principal management bargainer*
   1. Cost controls directly on principal and only bargainer.
   2. Controls on principal bargainer but not on manager involved if there is a failure to agree at that level.
   3. Controls on ratefixer/work study engineer but he is regularly over-ridden by the foreman.
   4. Controls no more than information on average earnings of sections.
   5. No controls at all.

Table 6:1 contains the results of a crude attempt at such a test.

For each of the ten factories studied, the Table provides an index of the state of certain areas of the management control system. The areas were selected because comprehensive data had been collected on them. They are fairly representative of the range of controls bearing upon piecework. The first area is the extent to which, in practice, waiting time is misrecorded. The second is the extent to which foremen have effective latitude to compensate workers for lost time or lost piecework earnings. The third area is the nature of the direct wage and cost controls bearing upon the principal management bargainer (or bargainers) in the piecework job value bargain. At some factories he is the work study engineer or ratefixer, at others he is the foreman and, at some places, if there is a failure to agree, another member of management may be brought in.

There are some emphatic reservations to be made about this test. It will be seen that the categories on the scale are not precise and in some cases depend upon somewhat impressionistic evaluations (notably where practice varies within a factory). Consequently any deductions from it are weak and it would be a nonsense to present statistical correlation coefficients.

The last two rows of the Table show the index of C&P leniency and the Topsy factor. The first point to be noticed is that, for each factory, there is a broad correspondence between the degree of management control recorded in each area. The second point is that both the index of C&P leniency and the Topsy factor correlate quite closely with the measures of management control. This is satisfactorily consistent with the hypothesis that management control systems are major determinants of the amount of non-negotiated drift both in C&P rules and in piecework wages.

THE EXTERNAL DETERMINANTS OF MANAGEMENT CONTROLS

The chain of causation that has been described in this

attempt to explain the operation of piecework bargaining has been long and one of its links remains to be explained. Management control systems have been given a central place both directly in affecting the growth of C&P and indirectly in influencing the degree of integration of the shop steward body and hence the degree of shop steward control over C&P. But it could be argued that, on the one hand, this leaves the determination of management control systems unclear and, on the other, that there could be a circular effect with strong and unconstitutional steward bodies battering management controls into disarray.

Both these criticisms deserve attention. The first one prompts the natural question of why, in fact, the control systems of different factories do differ so much. The second has some truth in it in that management control systems do suffer to some extent from the onslaughts of strong and 'bargaining aware' workforces, but this does not help the overall explanation very much. It is necessary to say something about the factors that determine the rigour of management control systems.

Dunlop's work prompts questions about the product and the production technology. Both these appear to be intuitively important. While one factory may appear to be obsessed with adhering to production deadlines but relatively careless of cost, another may be acutely cost conscious and yet another may put all emphasis upon the quality of its product. The technology of one factory may make work study a natural complement to other control systems and so facilitate piecework control; at another factory work study may be rendered impossible by the technology.

Assessment of the importance of these factors is made difficult by the notorious problems associated both with measuring competition and with analysing technologies. Measures of both concentration and of ease of entry are conceptually difficult in the context of individual product markets. Most of the firms studied had a product market share of at least one third and some did not appear to compete primarily in terms of price.

An illustration can be given by comparing factories A and B. They have very similar product technologies but very different product markets. For A, after-sales service and reputation were seen to be of greatest importance. A foreman there boasted that 'We don't sell the product; we allocate it' and his attitude to cost was typically casual. At the same time the product was expensive to hold in stock and this tended to give cost a still lower priority. For B, on the other hand, many products were made on a jobbing contracting basis for which careful tendering was necessary. Consequently, the work study engineers were given a much higher status within management and they found it easier to hold their own with foreman.

On the question of product technology, the two principal factors from the point of view of this discussion are, first, the proportion of the value added in the factory that arises from labour costs and, second, the extent to which the technology assists or hinders work study engineers. The relative importance of labour cost per unit of output needs little explanation. A firm's cost accountants will be much more likely to press for the control of a disorderly pay system if labour costs are a large proportion of value added than if they are a small one.

The characteristics of the production technology that influence the ease of work study are more complex. Accurate work study is made more possible if jobs are capable of being de-skilled, if batches are long, learning curves short, job elements short and interruptions rare. Work study is also strengthened if it is used for other management functions besides wage payment. If, for instance, (as was the case at H, J and K) it is important to production engineers for 'balancing' the flow of work on assembly lines, then work study engineers are likely to come under less pressure both from production engineers and from supervision. The close integration of work study into management controls in this way is likely to be accompanied by its use as a measure of labour inputs in a standard cost control system and as an accurate basis for tendering. All this will strengthen work study against the onslaughts of pieceworkers.

This has been the briefest of summaries of the major external factors influencing the management control of piecework. An account from which substantial generalizations could be made would be a major study in itself. Consequently, in attempting a quantitative test of the relationships described, this study will use very crude indicators for the different factors. These are set out in Table 6:2. A positive index reflects a factor that is likely to hinder strong controls, a negative one a factor that will help them and a zero indicates a neutral position. This Table should be treated with even more caution than its predecessors. The biggest qualifications to be made is that the indices are impressionistic. It is, as Lupton observed when he used a

TABLE 6:2

**The Characteristics of Product Market and
Production Technology**

TECHNICAL/MARKET CHARACTERISTIC	*A*	*B*	*C*	*D*	*E*	*F*	*G*	*H*	*J*	*K*
Price Competition not of Primary Importance	+1	−1	+1	+1	−1	+1	+1	0	0	−1
Production on Schedule of Importance	−1	0	+1	0	+1	+1	+1	+1	+1	+1
Quality/Precision more important than Price	+1	−1	0	+1	−1	0	0	−1	−1	0
Demand fluctuating and/or Inventories Costly	+1	+1	+1	−1	0	+1	+1	0	0	0
Labour cost as percentage of Value Added (≤55% +1, ≥65% −1)	0	0	+1	−1	+1	0	0	−1	−1	−1
Predominant Technology — Short Batch, Long, Individual	+1	+1	−1	−1	0	−1	−1	−1	−1	−1
Operations	+1	+1	−1	−1	−1	−1	−1	−1	−1	−1
High Skill	+1	+1	0	−1	−1	0	−1	−1	−1	−1
Crude total	+5	+2	+2	−3	−2	+1	0	−4	−4	−4
Crude Average Management Control Index	5·0	3·3	4·7	2·7	3·0	4·3	5·0	1·0	1·0	1·3
Index of C&P Leniency	4·7	3·7	4·3	2·2	2·8	3·5	4·5	1·2	1·3	1·2
Topsy Factor	83	79	81	57	65	77	81	20	45	35

similar table,[11] based on 'partial data and shaky generalizations'. Even the figures for labour costs as a proportion of value added, which are derived from the 1963 Census of Production, have the heavy qualification that average data for very broad industrial categories are applied to individual factories.

The first impression given by the Table is that the ten firms differ considerably in their technical and market characteristics. These indices are then summated as a crude total for each firm. Ignoring the gross problems of weighting that this raises, the crude total can then be compared with the index of the degree of management control derived in the last table. It will be seen that there is quite a strong positive correlation between them (it would be spurious to put this in numerical form) and this remains significant even when the three firms with tightly controlled piecework systems (H, J, and K) are omitted. Thus the test provides a result that is consistent with the hypothesis that the product market and the production technology are significant factors in determining the amount of control one can expect to find a management to have over its piecework system. It also suggests that the organizational and bargaining characteristics of the workforce are not the root causes of poor management controls; a weakly integrated workforce may exacerbate the weaknesses of a control system further but it will have been the initial inadequacy of the controls which made the integration of the shop steward body difficult in the first place.

It is important to put this argument in terms of expectations. Firms tend to remove their 'organizational slack' only when they are forced to do so. Thus, while one is more likely to find a firm with tight cost controls in a product market that is price competitive, there is nothing to prevent a similarly tightly controlled firm existing where costs are relatively unimportant. It is just less likely to happen.

The last two rows of the Table reproduce the C&P

[11] T. Lupton, *op. cit.*, pp. 194–201.

leniency and Topsy factor figures for each firm. It has been argued that the strength of management controls is the intervening variable between the externally determined characteristics of the factory and the amount of non-negotiated drift there is in both wages and rules. Consequently, it is not surprising that the index of product market and technology in Table 5:2 correlates with both the C&P leniency figure and the Topsy factor of each firm. These relationships also hold when firms H, J and K are omitted. This result reinforces confidence in the chain of causation that has been developed in this study, linking the characteristics of the product market at one end to the process of wage determination at the other. In doing so it helps explain the statistical relationship between wage movements and the product market that had been suggested by the analysis of Chapter Two.

Topsy Reconsidered

Although the causes and characteristics of non-negotiated bargaining have now been discussed at length, one question raised in Chapter Two remains to be answered. Why should non-negotiated wage drift be inherently more inflationary than negotiated drift? Evidence was presented to support the hypothesis that negotiated drift in piecework was essentially passive, providing compensatory increases in wages to restore differentials which non-negotiated drift had disturbed. In the light of the analysis of the last few chapters it is now possible to put forward a tentative explanation for the dominant role of non-negotiated wage drift in generating earnings increases. Three distinct mechanisms are evident.

The first mechanism arises from the facts that piecework bargaining is fragmented and frequent, and that individual bargains are conducted out of phase with each other. The statistical evidence of Chapter Three suggested that individual pieceworkers bargained in such a way as to maintain their historical differentials with respect to each other. This is equivalent to a situation in which everyone uses his bargaining opportunities to restore his earnings to his 'traditional' position expressed as a percentage of the average of the earnings of all pieceworkers in the factory. It is easy to demonstrate graphically that, if individuals bargain non-simultaneously, the average of all their earnings will increase faster as the frequency of their bargaining becomes greater. If they bargain in groups then not only the average frequency but also the degree of fragmentation of bargaining will affect the rate of non-negotiated wage drift. Chapter Four demonstrated that the frequency of bargaining was strongly influenced by the degree of leniency of C&P rules.

The second mechanism is that of the 'genetic analogy' drawn in Chapter Three. The greater the scatter of individual earnings within a piecework system, the greater is the scatter of the potential comparisons which an individual pieceworker might make use of during his own bargain. The more extravagant the comparisons which he can make, the larger the increase in earnings that will result from the bargain is likely to be. Thus, for a given frequency of bargaining, the greater the scatter of earnings, the greater the non-negotiated drift that can be expected to arise. It was noted in a footnote in Chapter Four that the scatter of earnings is positively associated with the leniency of C&P. It was also noted that more information on internal piecework earnings tends to be available in plants with high Topsy factors and lenient C&P.

The third reason for supposing non-negotiated drift to play a more active part in increasing earnings than negotiated drift arises from the different way in which power is used in the two processes. The outcome of an individual piecework bargain is always uncertain to the protagonists because of the difficulty of estimating the floor-to-floor times for jobs. As C&P rules become more lenient, pieceworkers become more able to control this uncertainty but they gain this power at the expense of their management opponent. It has already been noted that the pieceworker tends to bargain in such a way as to maintain his approximate historical position in the league table of individual earnings rather than so as simply to increase his earnings. The extra power that he gains from more lenient C&P will be used to increase the certainty that his historical position is maintained and he is likely to achieve this by gaining a slightly larger increase in earnings from the bargain than is strictly necessary. Since the same applies for all other pieceworkers in the same factory (or operating with the same C&P rules), the cumulative outcome will be a steady upward pressure on earnings.

Negotiated drift contrasts on all three of these points. Piecework negotiations are rarely carried out more often than annually and the time rates, base rates and conversion factors with which they are concerned are generally applicable to large groups of workers. Even when the shop steward committee is so poorly integrated that different groups of workers negotiate over their time rates separately, this is usually done in terms of an annual 'wage round' rather than by a succession of cumulative comparisons. A negotiation on a simple timerate has no effect upon the scatter of standard earnings of the workers concerned and negotiations over pieceworkers' base rates and conversion factors usually narrow the scatter of earnings. Finally, the impact of negotiations upon earnings is predictable. Consequently negotiators will be able to adjust precisely for any disturbance that has occurred to established differentials. As was argued in Chapter Five, stewards have a predisposition to act in this way in order to maintain good bargaining relationships and maximise their bargaining power.

In contrast to negotiated increases in pay, the increases in piecework earnings measured by the Topsy factor are self-propelling and not subject to collective control. This conclusion reinforces the central theme of this study: that wages cannot be explained by labour market competition alone; they are also political phenomena to be understood through political analysis of the processes of collective bargaining.

7
Conclusion

Piecework bargaining, like any other wage determination process, is influenced by both market forces and bargaining power. This study has attempted to demonstrate how they are linked. It has shown that, under relatively full employment, piecework wages have increasingly become insulated from changes in the state of the labour market. Bargaining power, on the other hand, influences wages in an immediate and obvious way and the relative bargaining power of management and workers is, in the first instance, determined by the rules governing the bargaining process. These rules are in turn heavily influenced by the control systems which managements see fit to install in their factories. However, the principal pressures influencing management control systems are those of the product market, and different product markets can vary considerably in both the degree and the character of their competitiveness. It is thus argued that, under relatively full employment and trade union organization, it is the product market rather than the labour market which has the major economic impact upon piecework wage determination.

The second main theme of the study has been the way in which bargaining power is used. Neither side can use its power fully or in a deliberate way unless it possesses some degree of unity. A weak control system gives rise to a management in which different factions so undermine each other that decisions, if taken at all, cannot be implemented. Similarly, whatever capacity for aggression a workforce may have, its shop stewards will be unable to undertake effective negotiations if it lacks political cohesion. In these conditions, Topsy will take over and both wages and work rules are liable to drift. Despite the apparent attractions of this drift in providing higher wages and greater unilateral control of work, shop stewards have a predisposition to oppose it. For their strongest interest is likely to be in making the maximum use of the collective power at their disposal in the pursuit of specific objectives.